REACHING YOUR MAXIMUM POTENTIAL... IN CHRIST

Bill Rudge

LIVING TRUTH PUBLISHERS

A Division of Bill Rudge Ministries, Inc.
Hermitage, Pennsylvania

REACHING YOUR MAXIMUM POTENTIAL IN CHRIST

Library of Congress Catalog Card Number: 98-065515
ISBN 1-889809-01-2

Copyright © 1983 by Bill Rudge
Updated and expanded edition copyright © 1998 by Bill Rudge

Published by Living Truth Publishers
A Division of Bill Rudge Ministries, Inc.
Hermitage, Pennsylvania

Printed in the United States of America

Contents

Introduction

It was in my first year of coaching soccer when I met Mike. Tryouts had just begun. As the skills of the new kids were being tested, we coaches gathered to observe. We were looking for raw talent — someone we could work with.

Then I spotted him. He was the heaviest and slowest kid on the field. None of the other coaches seemed interested, but I wanted him for my team because of the potential I saw in him. I wanted to train him and turn him into a great player.

The next two years our team won the championship, and Mike played a crucial role in it by putting into practice what we had trained him to do. He shut down the other teams' offense. He used his great size to power kick the ball down the field and in taking penalty and corner kicks. As a result, all the other coaches wanted him, and encouraged their "big" players to imitate him.

Mike went on to become an excellent wrestler and football player. He won the high school PIAA state heavyweight wrestling title in his senior year, and received a full football scholarship to the University of

Buffalo. While there he was a well respected standout in football and ranked nationally in wrestling — all the while maintaining dean's list academic standards.

Jesus Christ saw His disciples in this way. Though the growth of His Church did not depend solely with that group of ordinary people — its development was assured by the power of His Spirit and His sovereign design — yet, He chose to begin His work with weak and sinful people who later turned the world upside down for Him.

Jesus sees the same potential in us. Through the immeasurable power of His Word and Spirit, He continually works in us to fulfill His purpose as we give our lives to Him and live by the principles of His Word.

The two main goals of the Bill Rudge Ministries are:

1) to evangelize a spiritually searching world with the life-changing Gospel of Jesus Christ;

2) to challenge and motivate believers to reach their maximum potential in Christ by being Biblical Christians who walk in endurance and faithfulness until He returns.

You will discover in this book some of the dynamic Biblical principles that have tremendously impacted my life and molded my ministry. Jesus Christ can take an ordinary person and use him or her in an extraordinary way. That's what He did with me, as well as thousands of others who have accepted the challenge. As you apply these Biblical truths, I am certain that you too will begin to reach your maximum potential in Christ!

Examine the Evidence

With so many religious and philosophical options to choose from, why are you a Christian? Hopefully, it is because you are convinced that Jesus Christ is who He claims to be, and that the Bible is the unique revelation of God.

1 Peter 3:15 encourages us —

> But in your hearts set apart Christ as Lord. Always be prepared to give an answer to everyone who asks you to give the reason for the hope that you have. But do this with gentleness and respect.

Once I shared Christ with a young man to whom I was giving a ride. He said, "Bill, don't waste your time. I don't believe in Jesus Christ, and I don't believe in the Bible." I responded, "That's fine. You have a right to believe whatever you want, but don't be so foolish as to reject the Bible and Jesus Christ without first examining the overwhelming evidence."

I then shared with him some of the archaeological discoveries that have established the historical accuracy of innumerable Biblical details, as well as the scientific evidence, and the accuracy and superiority of Biblical health and nutrition principles.

I shared a few of the messianic prophecies in the Old Testament that had been made at least 400 years before Christ walked on earth, explaining the mathematical impossibility for anyone to fulfill just a few of these prophecies, yet Jesus fulfilled them all. I explained to him how the evidence of the resurrection is undeniable and asked him what other religious leader has an empty tomb.

I asked him to consider the numerous Biblical prophecies written almost 2,000 years ago concerning the last days in which we are now living — prophecies foretelling a one-world government, a one-world monetary system, and a one-world religion. The specific details and exactness of these and many other prophecies that are being fulfilled right before our eyes would have been impossible to foretell without divine inspiration.

Finally, I shared the reality of Jesus Christ through the tremendous way in which He has transformed my life and millions of others throughout history, as well as the miraculous interventions the Lord has done in my life and ministry. These evidences and many more, are the reasons why I totally gave my life to Christ!

Count the Cost

Once you are convinced that Jesus Christ is the promised Messiah, God uniquely manifest in the flesh, and the only way of salvation, you must count the cost before you give your life to Him. In Luke 14:28-33, Jesus shared the importance of counting the cost before following Him. He said one should not start building a tower without counting the cost, lest he run out of money and be ridiculed when unable to finish it. Should not a king about to go to war first consider whether he is able with 10,000 men to oppose a force of 20,000? In the same way, Jesus said, anyone who wants to be His disciple must count the cost of giving up everything for Him.

Before I was a Christian, I thought I was *god*. Not God the Creator, but *god* in the sense that I was invincible. I did some crazy things because of that philosophy. Deceived by the same lie Satan used on Adam and Eve, I was walking in rebellion against the one true God.

But I came to the realization that I was not *god* — that Jesus Christ was God's unique revelation of truth. He was the One I needed as my Savior and Lord.

I Had to Make a Choice

Once I examined the evidence, and was convinced who Christ is, I had to make a choice. Do I reject Him and walk away in self-deluded pride and rebellion, or do I humble myself, admit my rebellion, and trust in Him for my salvation?

By God's grace, I chose to give Christ my life. Making a 180-degree turn, I began following Him as Savior and Lord. It's called repentance. It's dying to self and living for Christ. We must dethrone self, quit playing God, and place Christ in His rightful position as Lord of our lives. Then His goals become our goals. His desires become our desires. His will becomes our will.

To illustrate, let's pretend you're on one trapeze and Jesus is on another. You have one hand holding on to your trapeze, and one hand holding on to Christ. You want to live for Christ, but you also want to live for self. You want to obey the Lord, but you also want to have your own will and do your own thing. You want Him to be your God, but you also want to be your own god. You want to run your own life, make your own decisions, have your own goals, and fulfill your own desires. But you can't hold on to both. Eventually the two trapeze bars go in opposite directions. If you try to both live for self and for the Lord, it will tear you apart.

That's why there are so many neurotic Christians walking around confused, depressed, and discouraged, not knowing what they believe or what God's will is. When Christians are only half-committed (trying to live for self and trying to live for the Lord) they are the most miserable people. They go out to witness and say, "Don't you want what I have?" The non-Christian says, "No thanks, I have enough problems already." And instead of impacting our world for Christ, as the first century believers did, we turn them off. That's why we'll never influence our world for Christ unless we ourselves are first totally sold out to Him.

There is no middle road. You can't straddle the fence. You must totally accept or reject Him. And to not totally accept Him is to reject Him. Revelation 3:16 says, "So, because you are lukewarm — neither hot nor cold — I am about to spit you out of My mouth." You must count the cost and then make a wise choice — total commitment to Christ as Lord!

Total Commitment

As I travel and minister throughout the U.S. and around the world, I find that many believers are not totally committed to the Lord. They do not realize the cost that they are going to pay in the near future, as the Lord's imminent return draws even nearer.

I want to challenge you to total commitment to Christ as Lord, so that God can prepare you to not only stand and endure, but to have greater power and victory than you have ever had in your walk with the Lord!

Heart Commitment

When I use the phrase total commitment, I'm not talking about what you say with your mouth, or what you appear to be on the surface. I'm talking about a heart commitment. I've learned from experience that outward appearances and words can be deceptive. Man looks at the externals, but God looks at the heart. Are your heart, your motives, your will, your goals, and your desires fully committed to Jesus Christ?

A lady who was a spiritualistic medium (today she would be called a trance channeler), claimed to believe the Bible was the Word of God, but she misquoted numerous Bible verses to back up her erroneous beliefs. After she finished speaking, I asked for an interview. I said, "Let's examine in context the Scriptures you quoted and see what they really say." As I exposed her Scripture twisting, she became irate and said, "I don't believe the Bible anyway. It is full of errors. It's all mythology." She confiscated the tape of the interview and threatened to wipe out our ministry. She believed and followed the Word of God whenever it was convenient. But when it went contrary to her own ideas, she discarded it.

Many Christians believe the Bible and live for the Lord as long as it poses no difficulty and goes along with their previously held beliefs. When it goes contrary to what they want to hear or do, they discard it and walk away in rebellion, or they compromise, or they attempt to twist it to express what they want it to say. Many *dip* into all the promises, all the blessings, all the miracles, and *skip* all the responsibilities, all the commitment, and all the obedience.

But for every gift and privilege God gives, there is a responsibility and a commitment:

- If you want the mountaintops, you've got to go through the valleys.

- If you want the benefits and blessings, you've got to make the commitment and pay the price.

- If you want the victories, you've got to fight the battles.

- If you want the gifts of the Spirit, you've got to develop the fruit of the Spirit.

- If you want the spiritual power, you've got to develop your spiritual muscles.

God Wants First Place

Throughout the Old Testament, God emphasized the principle that He wants first place in our lives. When He said to "Bring the whole tithe into the storehouse," He was saying, "I must be first in regard to your finances." When God said, "The seventh day is a Sabbath of the Lord your God. On it you shall not do any work," He was saying, "I must be first in regard to your time." When God said to "Bring the best of the firstfruits of your soil to the house of the Lord your God," He was saying, "I must be first in regard to your business and livelihood." When God asked for the firstborn of all cattle, He was saying, "I must be first in regard to your belongings." When God said, "You must give [consecrate] to Me the first-born of your sons," He was saying, "I must be first in regard to your family."

When Satan tempted Jesus by offering Him all the kingdoms of the world, he said, "All this I will give You, if You will bow down and worship me" (Matthew 4:9). Then Jesus said to him, "Away from Me, Satan! For it is written: 'Worship the Lord your God, and serve Him only'" (Matthew 4:10). Jesus clearly revealed that God not only wants first place, but He must be the only Lord and God in our lives.

Why does the Lord not allow anyone or anything else to be Lord and God in our lives? Not only because He created us and deserves that unique relationship, but He knows that anything or anyone else that controls our lives becomes our *god*. Eventually it will destroy us. In contrast David said, "Blessed are the people whose God is the Lord" (Psalm 144:15).

Take Up Your Cross

If you think total commitment is only for those in Christian leadership, look closer at Scripture. For example, Luke 14:25-27 says —

> Large crowds were traveling with Jesus, and turning to them He said: "If anyone comes to Me and does not hate his father and mother, his wife and children, his brothers and sisters — yes, even his own life — he cannot be My disciple. And anyone who does not carry his cross and follow Me cannot be My disciple."

Jesus is not saying we should literally hate our family or ourselves, or carry an actual cross around, but He is making it perfectly clear to the "large crowds" that to be His disciple requires total commitment!

The disciples knew full well what Christ meant when He said —

> If anyone would come after Me, he must deny himself and take up his cross and follow Me. For whoever wants to save his life will lose it, but whoever loses his life for Me and for the gospel will save it (Mark 8:34,35).

The disciples were well aware of the Roman crucifixions, and in their culture and context they knew Jesus was speaking about dying to self and total commitment of their lives to Him.

While ministering to the U.S. military in what was then West Germany, I also had an opportunity to speak in a large German house-church. Among the many West Germans and American GI's, there were also several people from East Germany, Russia, Poland, Romania, and Egypt. I spoke through an interpreter as I shared highlights of my testimony and the need to be totally committed in these last days. Many raised their hands to respond to the challenge.

I remained for over an hour following my message as I prayed and shared with several of the people. One man was from Egypt. He formerly was a Moslem, who spoke to us in broken English and German.

Between the interpreter and myself we were able to decipher what he said.

I learned that when he became a Christian, his Moslem family threw him off a train in an attempt to kill him, which resulted in the loss of his arm. This man, who had paid a tremendous price for giving his life to Christ, was not asking for prayer for his problems, but he was requesting that I pray for him to know and serve Jesus even more. This man had a strong desire to grow closer to the Lord, no matter what the cost — a desire all believers should have.

Bridge-Burning Commitment

Suppose you and I are in the military and our commanding officer says, "Up ahead is enemy territory and the only way to get there is by crossing this wooden bridge. Underneath that wooden bridge is a body of water infested with piranha, alligators, and poisonous snakes. But once we cross that bridge into enemy territory, we're going to burn the bridge behind us so there is no going back. It's either death or victory!"

That's the way it is when you give your life to Jesus Christ — you make a bridge-burning commitment. There's no going back. When I gave my life to Jesus Christ on May 23, 1971, I burned the bridges behind me. There's no going back to my old lifestyle.

Besides, if I would ever turn from the Lord, where would I go? Back to the martial arts to get involved in Eastern religions and the occult or the power of ki and ch'i? That's so inferior to Biblical Christianity that it's just not an option for me anymore.

Back to a pleasure-oriented existence, immorality, lust, and a violent lifestyle? None of that can compare to the fulfillment Jesus Christ has given me. It's not an option for me.

Could I return to pretending there is no God? How could I do that when I know the reality of the God of the Bible and have tasted of His goodness?

Perhaps I'd just become a New Ager and go with the flow, compromise Biblical Christianity and jump on the bandwagon with all the other "Christians" who think it's the moving of God's Spirit. But how could I deny God's genuine power, the truth of His Word, and the fulfillment that comes from knowing Him, a God who is so far above these inferior counterfeits?

So I'm in a dilemma. There is no other alternative for me. I've tried them all. I've evaluated them all. There's only one option for me, and that is Biblical Christianity!

Four Types of Commitment

I believe you are only as good as your word. That's why I do everything possible to keep mine. If you make a commitment to Christ today and then next week you have forgotten and given up, then it really wasn't much of a commitment. A real commitment is not just for one day or one week, but for the rest of your life. It is not just one or two hours on Sundays, but twenty-four hours a day, seven days a week. We should seek to live under His Lordship and glorify Him, not only when in church, reading our Bibles, praying or witnessing, but also when we are at work, engaged in sporting activities, working out at the gym, or anytime.

There are acceptable and unacceptable types of commitment mentioned in the Bible. Which of the following four categories is most like your commitment?

1) Outright Rebellion

Are you like King Ahab who, in outright rebellion against the Lord, did evil in His sight with no desire for repentance?

I Kings 16:29,30 —

> In the thirty-eighth year of Asa king of Judah, Ahab son of Omri became king of Israel, and he reigned in Samaria over Israel twenty-two years. Ahab son of Omri did more evil in the eyes of the Lord than any of those before him.

Though Ahab was king of the northern tribes of Israel, he openly rebelled against God. There are many who name the name of Jesus Christ outwardly, but according to God's Word, in their hearts they are in outright rebellion by the way they live and the things in which they are involved.

2) Halfheartedly

Do you serve the Lord halfheartedly like Amaziah, king of Judah?

II Chronicles 25:1,2 —

> Amaziah was twenty-five years old when he became king, and he reigned in Jerusalem twenty-nine years. His mother's name was Jehoaddin; she was from Jerusalem. He did what was right in the eyes of the Lord, but not wholeheartedly.

3) Wholeheartedly — But Not All Your Life

Do you serve the Lord wholeheartedly, but have not maintained that commitment your whole life? Like Uzziah, king of Judah, when the Lord blessed and he became powerful, then he became proud and turned away from the Lord.

II Chronicles 26:3-5,16 —

> Uzziah was sixteen years old when he became king, and he reigned in Jerusalem fifty-two years. ... He did what was right in the eyes of the Lord, just as his father Amaziah had done. He sought God during the days of Zechariah, who instructed him in the fear of God. As long as he sought the Lord, God gave him success. But after Uzziah became powerful, his pride led to his downfall. He was unfaithful to the Lord his God, and entered the

temple of the Lord to burn incense on the altar of incense.

So far we have three types of commitment: those who live in outright rebellion and do evil before the Lord; those who only halfheartedly serve the Lord; and those who wholeheartedly serve the Lord, but only for a short duration. They run the race for maybe two, three, five, or ten years, and then they get weary and fall into rebellion and sin.

4) Wholeheartedly — All Your Life

Are you like Abraham, Moses, Caleb, Ruth, David, Elijah, Daniel, and Paul, who all made a commitment to serve the Lord, and served Him wholeheartedly all the days of their lives? It is this kind of commitment God desires from the body of Christ this day.

Consider the challenging words David spoke to his son Solomon —

> And you, my son Solomon, acknowledge the God of your father, and serve Him with wholehearted devotion and with a willing mind, for the Lord searches every heart and understands every motive behind the thoughts. If you seek Him, He will be found by you; but if you forsake Him, He will reject you forever (I Chronicles 28:9).

Don't just serve the Lord halfheartedly all your life — or even wholeheartedly half your life. Instead, serve the Lord wholeheartedly all of your life!

When I was on a speaking tour in Tobago, a small island in the West Indies, I was informed that there are two main waterfalls on the island. To get to one takes an easy two or three minute walk. Although it's nice, the other one is far more beautiful, but would require a 45-minute walk through streams, over stones and rocks, across slippery ledges, and through thick brush.

Having a few hours of free time, my ministry team decided to go with me on the longer excursion. I had to go barefoot because I loaned someone else my shoes. The bottoms of my feet were so sore the next day from walking over all the stones that I could hardly walk, but it was well worth the effort. The waterfall was awesome, forming three tiers of pools. When we swam in the cool and refreshing waters it was like being in paradise.

Most people visiting Tobago avoid the more difficult way and are satisfied just to see the first falls. As one who is willing to pay the price for that which is truly worthwhile, I led the team into a breathtaking area that was unsurpassed in beauty and serenity instead of settling for second best.

Too many people are willing to settle for convenient Christianity. But the real blessings, power, and victories are manifested in the lives of those who are totally committed to the Lord with all their hearts. Believe me, it is well worth it!

Gave My All

Before I was a Christian, I was totally dedicated to weightlifting, karate, and the pursuit of pleasure. I gave 100% commitment to serving myself. How much more should I give my life totally to the King of Kings and Lord of Lords?

You see, I'm an "all or nothing" person. I either want to go all the way with the Lord or not at all. Anything less is really not Biblical Christianity. If I'm going to serve Christ, my desire is to serve Him with all my heart, with all my mind, and with all my strength. I will not settle for a superficial Christianity. I want everything God has for me. And I believe you do, too. In this age of apostasy and compromise, God is raising up a body of believers whose desire is to no longer live a nominal, superficial, imitation Christianity, but to be totally committed to the Lord and walk in sensitivity and obedience to His Word and His Spirit.

Before I gave my life to Christ, I learned to use almost every part of my body as a weapon. I learned to use my hands, feet, knees, elbows, fingers, and wrists as destructive weapons. Should I not now seek to use every aspect of my life to glorify the Lord?

His Lordship affects everything I do and how I live. It affects:

- what my eyes see
- what my mouth speaks
- what my ears listen to
- what my hands do
- where my feet go
- what my mind thinks
- what attitudes I have
- what emotions I tolerate
- what my heart desires
- how I take care of my body
  (the temple of the Holy Spirit)

His Lordship affects every aspect of my life — physically, mentally/emotionally, and spiritually.

Have I Achieved Perfection?

Have I achieved perfection? Not in this life. Do I struggle with sin and temptation? We all do. In this world we are never going to achieve perfection. I'm not trying to be a pious, self-righteous person. If you would follow me around you would see flaws and imperfections in my life, but you would have to admit that the sincere desire of my heart is to totally live for and glorify the Lord and fulfill His purpose for my life and ministry. My righteousness is not through self-righteousness but through the righteousness of God's Son, Jesus Christ. My salvation is solely based on faith, not works or self-effort.

As I indicate from Scripture in my pamphlet entitled, *What Is A Christian?*, we become Christians totally and completely by God's grace and mercy through faith. And, as Paul reveals in Galatians 3:2- 5, we *continue* to live by faith after we are saved.

Paul states in Galatians 5 —

> It was for freedom that Christ set us free [from unsuccessfully trying to fulfill the law to earn our salvation]; therefore keep standing firm and do not be subject again to a yoke of slavery. For you were called to freedom, brethren; only do not turn your freedom into an opportunity for the flesh. ... Now those who belong to Christ Jesus have crucified the flesh with its passions and desires. If we live by the Spirit, let us also walk by the Spirit (Galatians 5:1,13,24,25 - NAS).

Therefore, we must achieve a balanced under- standing between God's grace and our responsibility to be committed to His Lordship, and walk in obedience to His Word and Spirit.

Had to Grow

After I gave my life to Christ, I had to grow. Sure, I have fallen and failed many times since making a total commitment, but I didn't quit or lie there and give up in defeat. I asked for forgiveness, and by God's grace, got back up and kept on going.

I John 2:1 (which was written to believers) says —

> I am writing these things to you that you may not sin. And if anyone sins, we have an advocate with the Father, Jesus Christ the righteous (NAS).

And I John 1:9 (which was also written to believers) states —

> If we confess our sins, He is faithful and just and will forgive us our sins and purify us from all unrighteousness.

If a Sheep Falls in the Mud

I used to struggle with such questions as, "Do we just go ahead and fall into sin because we have these

Scriptural promises of forgiveness and liberty in Christ, or do we attempt to live a legalistic lifestyle trying to achieve perfection?"

A professor at Bible college helped answer that with the following illustration. He explained that if a pig falls in the mud, it lies there and wallows in it because that is according to its nature. But if a sheep falls in the mud, it gets out, because it is contrary to its nature to lie there and wallow in it. So too, a non-believer may wallow and continue in sin without any remorse or guilt, while believers who fall into sin will repent and come out of it as God's Spirit deals with them and speaks to their hearts.

If you continue in willful sin, then you had better re-evaluate your relationship with the Lord. I'm not talking about making mistakes. But if you have a pattern of continual, willful sin, and you know that it's wrong before the Lord, then you had better re-examine your commitment to the Lord. I John 3:6 says —

> No one who lives in Him keeps on sinning. No one who continues to sin has either seen Him or known Him.

Feelings Change like the Weather

Realize that our commitment to Jesus Christ must not be based on feelings. I don't always feel like praying. I don't always feel like reading my Bible. I don't always feel like doing what God wants. Sure I get discouraged and want to give up, but nowhere does the Bible say we should base our relationship with Christ on feelings. We walk and live by faith and obedience to God's Word and Spirit.

I feel great when the Lord blesses, but even when it appears He's not blessing and even when things are going wrong, I still serve Him. My feelings may change like the weather, but my commitment to Him is unchanging!

Walk in Obedience

Throughout the Old and New Testaments we meet people who offered sacrifices and went through all the outward appearances of spirituality. But God said they were uncircumcised in heart, disobedient, stiff-necked, and rebellious. Why? Because God is concerned with the attitude of the heart more than with external displays. God desires a people who are obedient and faithful.

King Saul learned the hard way that to obey is better than sacrifice. Following Saul's lame excuse for only partially obeying the Lord's command, the prophet Samuel rebuked him with the following words —

> Does the Lord delight in burnt offerings and sacrifices as much as in obeying the voice of the Lord? To obey is better than sacrifice, and to heed is better than the fat of rams. For rebellion is like the sin of divination, and arrogance like the evil of idolatry. Because you have rejected the word of the Lord, He has rejected you as king (1 Samuel 15:22,23).

It is very important that we not only talk our Christianity, but that we also walk it. Titus 1:16 states —

> They claim to know God, but by their actions

they deny Him. They are detestable, disobedient and unfit for doing anything good.

All through the Scriptures we meet those who were tempted, tested, and confronted by obstacles. Some rebelled, disobeyed, and turned from the Lord, while others remained faithful no matter what the cost. Those who disobeyed, either immediately or in the not-too-distant future, suffered the consequences, while those who obeyed ultimately received great blessing and victory.

Obey without Talking Back

When I was in gymnastics and my instructor said, "Bill, climb the rope to the gym's ceiling. Do a round off and several backhand springs in a row on the mat. Get on the trampoline and do a double back flip." I didn't say, "I don't feel like doing that today." I did it!

When I went out for football and the coach said, "Hit the sled and keep hitting it until I tell you to stop. Run the ropes. Take five laps." I didn't say, "Well coach, I'm not in the mood to do that today." I did it!

When I was in karate and my instructor said, "Do knuckle pushups." I did knuckle pushups. When he said, "You, Rudge, come here. I want to use you for an *uke* and beat on you for awhile." I didn't say, "Not today, sensei, maybe next time." No, I stepped forward and let him beat on me. When he said spar and fight, I sparred and fought!

Should I obey any less the King of Kings and Lord of Lords, the God who created me, the God who came and died for me, who bodily rose from the dead, and who is coming again soon to rule and reign for all eternity?

When His Word and Spirit tell me to do something, how much more should I obey without talking back or whining or complaining or making excuses? I don't say, "Well, if I feel like it, Lord," or

"Maybe I'll think about it," or "I don't know if I want to do that." I obey! That's what it means to be submitted to Christ's Lordship.

You may say, "Is that Biblical?" In Luke 6:46-49 Jesus states —

> Why do you call Me, "Lord, Lord," and do not do what I say? I will show you what he is like who comes to Me and hears My words and puts them into practice. He is like a man building a house, who dug down deep and laid the foundation on rock. When a flood came, the torrent struck that house but could not shake it, because it was well built. But the one who hears My words and does not put them into practice is like a man who built a house on the ground without a foundation. The moment the torrent struck that house, it collapsed and its destruction was complete.

In John 14:15 Jesus said, "If you love Me, you will obey what I command."

In Matthew 7:21 Jesus states —

> Not everyone who says to Me, "Lord, Lord," will enter the kingdom of heaven, but only he who does the will of My Father who is in heaven.

I John 2:3-6 says —

> And by this we know that we have come to know Him, if we keep His commandments. The one who says, "I have come to know Him," and does not keep His commandments, is a liar, and the truth is not in him; but whoever keeps His word, in him the love of God has truly been perfected. By this we know that we are in Him: the one who says he abides in Him ought himself to walk in the same manner as He walked (NAS).

And the manner in which He walked was in humility and obedience (Philippians 2:8).

Surrendered and Available

Once you give your life to Jesus Christ, God begins to work in and through you to accomplish His will. Philippians 1:6 says, "Being confident of this, that He who began a good work in you will carry it on to completion until the day of Christ Jesus." Philippians 2:13 states, "For it is God who works in you to will and to act according to His good purpose." I Thessalonians 5:24 promises, "The One who calls you is faithful and He will do it."

You Have Two Choices — Submit or Resist

The choice is yours. Either you submit and say, "Here I am, Lord. Use me to accomplish Your will, Your goals, and Your purpose." God then molds you, leads you, and enables you to accomplish His purpose. Or you resist, becoming stiff-necked, obstinate, hardhearted, and rebellious as you struggle against the free reign of God's Spirit in your life. Then you will not be used to bear fruit in Christ's Kingdom or to achieve the full potential and purpose He has for you. Will you be submissive and surrendered or resistant and rebellious?

Isaiah heard the voice of the Lord ask, "Whom shall I send, and who will go for Us?" His response was, "Here am I. Send me!" (6:8). Isaiah went on to become one of the greatest Biblical prophets.

When I first started our ministry, I was no speaker and couldn't write. The odds were not in my favor. I had no hope and no real potential. So I prayed: "Lord, here I am, I yield myself to You. No matter what it costs, I'm willing to do Your will!" God has molded my life and ministry over the years — often in the desert and wilderness of adversity. He has used my books, pamphlets, cassettes, speaking engagements, and radio broadcasts to impact the lives of tens of thousands of people around the world.

Two Attitudes

As I deal with Christians involved in a variety of questionable or blatantly unscriptural practices, I find they have one of two attitudes.

First, some respond: "I really don't care what you say or how much evidence you have concerning the potential danger or what God's Word says about it." They become defensive and somehow try to justify or condone their involvement. As long as they have this attitude, God cannot guide and direct them to accomplish His purpose.

II Chronicles 30:7,8 was a warning sent throughout Israel and Judah by King Hezekiah. It stated —

> Do not be like your fathers and brothers, who were unfaithful to the Lord, the God of their fathers, so that He made them an object of horror, as you see. Do not be stiff-necked, as your fathers were; submit to the Lord ....

Stephen echoed a similar rebuke which resulted in his being stoned. In Acts 7:51 he cried out —

> You stiff-necked people, with uncircumcised hearts and ears! You are just like your fathers: You always resist the Holy Spirit!

27

Proverbs 29:1 states —

A man who remains stiff-necked after many rebukes will suddenly be destroyed — without remedy.

But the second attitude, the one God desires us all to have, is that of saying, "Father, I want Your will for my life more than anything else. I may not see anything visibly wrong with what I'm doing, but I'll read and search Your Word. I'll get on my knees and pray and fast and be sensitive, submissive, and obedient to what Your Word and Your Spirit lead me to do."

Don't Condemn

As I talk to non-Christians, I do not condemn their music, alcohol, smoking, sexual promiscuity, occult activities, and so on. I may warn them about potential consequences, but I do not condemn them, because even though they cease that involvement, they are still lost without Christ. I share the overwhelming evidence for Jesus Christ and the superior peace, joy, and power that is available through the resurrected Christ!

Don't let the enemy get us sidetracked dealing with peripheral issues. Remember, the Lord Jesus did not enter Jerusalem and cleanse Pilate's judgment hall or Herod's palace, but He did cleanse the temple. Besides, when non-Christians come to faith in Christ and are truly submitted to Him as Lord, His Spirit and Word will begin to transform their lifestyle.

However, when I deal with Christians who are involved in unscriptural activities — that's different. I let them know that they need to clean up their lives, and I challenge them to become sensitive and obedient to God's Spirit and Word.

One Reassuring Fact

A Christian lady, who was involved in a questionable practice that was potentially dangerous spiritually, felt God was leading her to quit, although she didn't know why. She saw nothing visibly wrong with it. After talking with her, I shared some facts that she was not aware of. Tears began to flow down her face as she said, "You have confirmed what God's Spirit has been speaking to my heart." As a result of her sensitivity and submission to the Lord, He was able to protect her from a dangerous practice and lead her in the path He desired for her life.

It is reassuring to know that when you remain yielded, available, and surrendered to God, it is impossible for you to get too far out of line. If you get involved with a practice or belief that is unacceptable to Him, He will speak to your heart through His Word and Spirit, and the Great Shepherd will guide and direct you back to the path of righteousness.

The problem starts when you become insensitive, stiff-necked, obstinate, and hard-hearted, or try to justify your involvement. Then you get out of God's will and resist His Spirit's dealings with you.

When you have this kind of rebellious attitude before the Lord, you have one promise — that of reaping what you have sown. But when you are sensitive and yielded to the Spirit of God and obedient to His Word, you have a promise of eventual blessing, victory, and all things working together for good. You will be aware of God working in your life and using you to achieve the purpose and potential He has for you.

Almost Hit by Bus in the Himalayas

After speaking at a convention in the Himalayas of northern India, our missions team and I were making our way down the winding mountain roads as we headed to Calcutta. We stopped in the village of Darjeeling. Standing in the middle of a narrow road for a more panoramic view, my son and I were surveying this Himalayan mountain village to decide in which direction we wanted to go. Suddenly a bus came speeding around a sharp curve heading straight toward us. Horn blaring, the bus maintained its speed as it drew nearer and nearer with no sign of slowing down.

Quickly I sized up the situation, glancing to my right and left. Instinctively, I grabbed B.J., my thirteen-year-old son, and swiftly tried pulling him to the left, but his impulsive reaction was to go in the opposite direction. I quickly adjusted my momentum to accommodate his motion by pushing him to the right. He simultaneously responded to my initial tug by moving toward the left. There we were in the middle of the road going in circles as this massive bus came bearing down upon us. I could have jumped out of the way and saved my life, but I promised my wife I'd bring our son back alive. If he was going to die, then I was going to die with him on the streets of India, so I hung on to him.

B.J. was in a near panic, and I wasn't doing real well myself. With adrenaline flowing and my heart pounding, thoughts of how we were both going to be killed flooded my mind, because buses in India are notorious for not stopping for pedestrians. I personally have seen them barreling down the road, stopping for no one as hundreds of people step aside or leap to safety seconds before the bus speeds by, sometimes missing them by inches.

Realizing this, our situation seemed hopeless. Fortunately, by the grace of God, the driver must have realized we really were in trouble, and to our amazement, he suddenly slammed on the brakes and slid to a stop no more than two feet in front of us.

I remember standing there in the middle of the

street after it was all over and looking at the flat front of the bus directly ahead of me thinking, "I couldn't have even jumped on its hood to get thrown to the side. It would have hit us, dropped us in the street, and then run over us. We would have had no hope for survival." Thank God for His mercy and protection!

The point of this illustration is that when our heavenly Father is leading us in one direction, and we are insisting on going in another, then dangerous, and sometimes fatal consequences occur. Rather than going around in circles in your life, get your lead from the Lord.

Four Options

When I was involved in the martial arts before the Lord led me out, the easiest way for me to lead someone's body was to lead their head. Wherever their head went, their body would follow. I used to demonstrate this with a volunteer from the audience.

Now it was easy to lead a person who was submissive and yielded. But if they would stiffen their neck and resist, I would explain that I had a few basic choices:

1) I could exert more force and possibly injure his neck.

2) I could break his stiff neck.

3) I could knock him unconscious and then drag him wherever I wanted.

4) Or, I could let him go his own way and bang his head against the wall, or against my knee, or whatever, as a natural consequence of his resistance.

When we resist the Lord's will and refuse to submit, He also has choices:

1) He can exert more pressure in our lives to get our attention.

2) He can break our stiff necks and rebellious wills by humbling us.

3) He can knock us unconscious by not using us anymore, or He can allow Satan to render us ineffective.

4) Or, He will let us go our own rebellious ways and reap the consequences, until we learn and are ready to submit.

What Do Meekness and a Strong Horse Have in Common?

Throughout the Scriptures we frequently see the word "meek." Many wrongly equate the meaning of meek with its rhyming word weak. But that could not be further from the truth. When the Lord said in Matthew 5:5, "Blessed are the meek, for they will inherit the earth," He was talking about those who will rule and reign with Him.

While in Bible college, I learned that the word meek was used in the Greek in reference to a strong war horse which was prepared for battle. With just the slightest touch on the reins, the horse would go in the intended direction of the rider. It became submissive and sensitive to the rider on its back. The horse had not lost any of its drive or dynamic power as a strong stallion, but had merely been brought under the mastery of the one who rode on its back. If its spirit was broken, its strength drained, or any of its dynamic quality changed, then it would be useless for its purpose. But as it was brought under control and submission, it was said that the horse was now *praus*, translated meek (or *prautes*, translated meekness) throughout the New Testament.

Vine's Expository Dictionary states:

It is that temper of spirit in which we accept His [God's] dealings with us as good, and therefore without disputing or resisting; and as such, we do not fight ... struggle and contend with Him .... It must be clearly understood, therefore, that the meekness manifested by the Lord and commended to the believer is the fruit of power. The common assumption is that when a man is meek it is because he cannot help himself; but the Lord was "meek" because He had the infinite resources of God at His command.

Isaiah 45:5,9 declares —

I am the Lord, and there is no other; apart from Me, there is no God. ... Woe to him who quarrels with his Maker. ... Does the clay say to the potter, "What are you making?"

I went horseback riding as a teen, and the horse I was riding was determined to knock me off. It tried to smash my legs by continually running about two inches from the trees. I had to keep pulling one of my feet out of the stirrups and lift my leg over to the other side of the saddle to avoid having it smashed against a tree. When that didn't work, the horse tried to "clothesline" me a few times by going underneath low branches. I had to keep ducking down to avoid getting knocked off.

There I was on this out-of-control horse! I was pulling as hard as I could on the reins in an attempt to stop it or even slow it down — so hard that its mouth was bleeding. But it would not stop; it ran even faster and tried all the harder to knock me off.

This horse finally got so upset with me trying to slow it down, that it impulsively ran off the trail and burst through a barbed-wire fence as it headed back to the corral. Its chest had multiple gashes causing blood mixed with sweat to run down. My pants were ripped and my legs had several cuts.

That horse was rebellious. I could not control or lead it. God does not want you to be like that horse because you will bring destruction on yourself. He says to be meek, humble, and yielded so He can work in you; so He can speak to your heart and lead you where He wants, without having to hit you over the head to get your attention or to force you to obey.

Psalm 32:9 states —

> Do not be as the horse or as the mule which have no understanding, whose trappings include bit and bridle to hold them in check ... (NAS).

Now the *praus* horse also had a bit and bridle, but to get it to obey one didn't have to yank the reins and bit or bloody its mouth. Rather, one lightly pulled on the reins to guide and direct the horse. It willingly followed the master's direction.

God is not telling us to be weak or a doormat. He's saying, "Have your dynamic strength, but don't resist and fight Me. Be submitted to Me."

Instead of being stiff-necked, obstinate, hard-hearted, and rebellious, let's be *praus.* Let's be sensitive, submissive, surrendered, yielded, and available so God will work in and through us to accomplish His purpose for our lives!

Evaluate Your Motives

One of the surest ways to fall is to allow pride to rule your life. Satan fell because of pride and self-glorification, which caused him to lose his position in God's presence. He enjoys seeing others fail in this same area.

God's Word has much to say concerning pride and arrogance. Let me share just a few examples. "I hate pride and arrogance" (Proverbs 8:13). "When pride comes, then comes disgrace" (Proverbs 11:2). "Before his downfall a man's heart is proud" (Proverbs 18:12). "I will put an end to the arrogance of the haughty and will humble the pride of the ruthless" (Isaiah 13:11).

Scripture is not talking about pride which motivates us to strive for excellence, to be the best that we can be, to stand in confidence and boldness and obedience to the Lord, or to boast in the Lord as the Apostle Paul did. It is referring to the kind of pride that is haughty, rebellious, self-willed, self-centered, self-glorifying, and boasts in the flesh. This type of pride always ends in defeat and destruction.

Examples of Pride

Chapters 36 and 37 in Isaiah give an amazing account of pride that led to a fall, and humility that resulted in honor. Sennacherib, king of Assyria, laid siege to the cities of Judah. He sent his field commander to Jerusalem to intimidate King Hezekiah into surrendering. The field commander made such boasts as —

> Hear the words of the great king, the king of Assyria! This is what the king says: Do not let Hezekiah deceive you. He cannot deliver you! Do not let Hezekiah persuade you to trust in the Lord when he says, "The Lord will surely deliver us; this city will not be given into the hand of the king of Assyria." Has the god of any nation ever delivered his land from the hand of the king of Assyria? Who of all the gods of these countries has been able to save his land from me? How then can the Lord deliver Jerusalem from my hand? (Isaiah 36:13-15,18,20).

Hezekiah went into the temple of the Lord in humility and spread out a letter containing more of Sennacherib's threats and boasting (Isaiah 37:10-14) as he prayed —

> O Lord Almighty, God of Israel, enthroned between the cherubim, You alone are God over all the kingdoms of the earth. You have made heaven and earth. Give ear, O Lord, and hear; open Your eyes, O Lord, and see; listen to all the words Sennacherib has sent to insult the living God. It is true, O Lord, that the Assyrian kings have laid waste all these peoples and their lands. They have thrown their gods into the fire and destroyed them, for they were not gods but only wood and stone, fashioned by human hands. Now, O Lord our God, deliver us from his hand, so that all kingdoms on earth may know that You alone, O Lord, are God (Isaiah 37:16-20).

Isaiah 37:36-38 gives the end result —

> Then the angel of the Lord went out and put to death a hundred and eighty-five thousand men in the Assyrian camp. When the people got up the next morning — there were all the dead bodies! So

Sennacherib king of Assyria broke camp and withdrew. He returned to Nineveh and stayed there. One day, while he was worshiping in the temple of his god Nisroch, his sons Adrammelech and Sharezer cut him down with the sword ....

Nebuchadnezzar was king of the powerful Babylonian empire. He saw that Daniel, inspired by the God of the Bible, was able not only to interpret his dream, but also to tell him what his dream was, when the astrologers and wise men of Babylon could not (Daniel 2). On another occasion Nebuchadnezzar witnessed the protection of Shadrach, Meshach, and Abednego, the three young Hebrew men he had thrown into the fiery furnace for not bowing down and worshiping his golden image (Daniel 3). Nevertheless, his heart remained proud. We read his arrogant words in Daniel 4:30 —

Is not this the great Babylon I have built as the royal residence, by my mighty power and for the glory of my majesty?

Archaeological excavations reveal that Nebuchadnezzar's Babylon was truly incredible.

Daniel 4:31-33 continues —

The words were still on his lips when a voice came from heaven, "This is what is decreed for you, King Nebuchadnezzar: Your royal authority has been taken from you. You will be driven away from people and will live with the wild animals; you will eat grass like cattle. Seven times will pass by for you until you acknowledge that the Most High is sovereign over the kingdoms of men and gives them to anyone He wishes."

Immediately what had been said about Nebuchadnezzar was fulfilled. He was driven away from people and ate grass like cattle. His body was drenched with the dew of heaven until his hair grew like the feathers of an eagle and his nails like the claws of a bird.

However, after seven years of humiliation we read

the following account in Daniel 4:34-37 —

> At the end of that time, I, Nebuchadnezzar, raised my eyes toward heaven, and my sanity was restored. Then I praised the Most High; I honored and glorified Him who lives forever. His dominion is an eternal dominion; His kingdom endures from generation to generation. All the peoples of the earth are regarded as nothing. He does as He pleases with the powers of heaven and the peoples of the earth. No one can hold back His hand or say to Him: "What have You done?"
>
> At the same time that my sanity was restored, my honor and splendor were returned to me for the glory of my kingdom. My advisers and nobles sought me out, and I was restored to my throne and became even greater than before. Now I, Nebuchadnezzar, praise and exalt and glorify the King of heaven, because everything He does is right and all His ways are just. And those who walk in pride He is able to humble.

In Acts 12:21-23, we read of an account in which Herod did not fare as well as Nebuchadnezzar —

> On the appointed day Herod, wearing his royal robes, sat on his throne and delivered a public address to the people. They shouted, "This is the voice of a god, not of a man." Immediately, because Herod did not give praise to God, an angel of the Lord struck him down, and he was eaten by worms and died.

II Thessalonians 2:4 indicates that the Antichrist will exalt himself above all that is called God or that is worshiped. He will speak proud words and blasphemies and slander God's name. He will compel the inhabitants of the earth to worship him (Revelation 13:5-8). But his haughtiness will only last for forty-two months (Revelation 13:5), as his humiliating defeat will occur at the Second Coming of Christ (II Thessalonians 2:8) when he is thrown into the lake of fire (Revelation 19:20).

King Saul fell because of pride and arrogance. He thought it intolerable that David, a young sheepherder, could detract from his popularity. Puffed up by pride and blinded by jealousy, Saul on numerous occasions disobeyed the Lord. This resulted in his eventual judgment and destruction.

George Armstrong Custer once boasted that his 7th Cavalry alone could whip all the Indians on the Plains. But on a hot Sunday in June of 1867, the Battle of Little Bighorn was "Custer's Last Stand."

Throughout the years I have seen many come on the scene who brag and boast about their physical strength or skills, their popularity, possessions, success, power, and so on. Often, however, within a few years (sometimes months, weeks, or even days) their haughty words are quieted by failure, humiliation, an injury, degenerative disease, tragic accident, the onset of old age, etc.

There are countless illustrations throughout history of skeptics, atheists, dictators, rock stars, athletes, and many others who became proud, and brazenly boasted and bragged in the flesh — for a while. Eventually their tongues were silenced. The historical records are strewn with the tragedies of these people.

How wise the advice of the Psalmist —

> Do not put your trust in princes, in mortal men, who cannot save. When their spirit departs, they return to the ground; on that very day their plans come to nothing (Psalm 146:3,4).

How true the words of Proverbs 16:18 —

> Pride goes before destruction, a haughty spirit before a fall.

And how accurate the statement of I John 2:17 —

> The world and its desires pass away, but the man who does the will of God lives forever.

Overcome Bragging

In my walk with the Lord, I have noticed a very definite pattern. Every time I would get a little too "puffed up," brag too much, or become overconfident in the flesh, it wasn't very long before I would be humbled. When I would truly humble myself before the Lord and keep my mouth shut, He would eventually honor me. Having realized this pattern, and being convinced it was truly the Lord's doing, I have strongly attempted to overcome pride and bragging — and boast only in the Lord.

Matthew 23:12 states —

> For whoever exalts himself will be humbled, and whoever humbles himself will be exalted.

Proverbs 22:4 says —

> Humility and the fear of the Lord bring wealth and honor and life.

Christ Humbly Obeyed

Isaiah 14:13,14 says concerning the king of Babylon (who many believe is a reference to Satan) —

> You said in your heart, "I will ascend to heaven; I will raise my throne above the stars of God; I will sit enthroned on the mount of assembly, on the utmost heights of the sacred mountain. I will ascend above the tops of the clouds; I will make myself like the Most High."

Nevertheless, God said, "But you are brought down to the grave, to the depths of the pit" (Isaiah 14:15). In contrast, Philippians 2:5-8 states, regarding Christ —

> Your attitude should be the same as that of Christ Jesus: Who, being in very nature God, did not consider equality with God something to be grasped, but made Himself nothing, taking the very nature of a servant, being made in human likeness. And being found in appearance as a man, He

humbled Himself and became obedient to death —
even death on a cross.

As a result of this, the outcome is the exact
opposite of what happened to Satan (Revelation
12:9). Philippians 2:9 -11 states —

> Therefore God exalted Him to the highest place
> and gave Him the name that is above every name,
> that at the name of Jesus every knee should bow,
> in heaven and on earth and under the earth, and
> every tongue confess that Jesus Christ is Lord, to
> the glory of God the Father.

Moses — A Great Leader

Moses was a great leader. For example, his
humility and selflessness was clearly seen when he
was informed by the Lord that he was about to die.
He was not troubled for himself, but for the people he
had so faithfully led throughout the years. Numbers
27:15-17 states —

> Moses said to the Lord, "May the Lord, the God
> of the spirits of all mankind, appoint a man over
> this community to go out and come in before them,
> one who will lead them out and bring them in, so
> the Lord's people will not be like sheep without a
> shepherd."

Instead of leaving the people in disarray in hopes
they would see how much they needed him and what
a great leader he had been, Moses' was concerned for
the well-being of the people God had entrusted into
his care. Moses desired God to raise up an adequate
replacement for him who would succeed and not fail.

On a previous occasion, Moses was more
concerned about God's reputation and that His name
did not fall into reproach than for his own success
and honor (Numbers 14:12-19). No wonder Numbers
12:3 says of him, "Now Moses was a very humble
man, more humble than anyone else on the face of
the earth."

Judgment Seat of Christ

Scripture reveals that believers will appear before the judgment seat of Christ (II Corinthians 5:10), not for our sins (John 5:24; Romans 8:1), but for our motives and how we used our talents. Romans 14:12 makes it very clear that, "each of us will give an account of himself to God." The motives for everything we *supposedly* did for His honor will be exposed. Only that which we *really* did for His glory and not our own will endure. The rest will be burned as wood, hay, or straw (I Corinthians 3:11-15).

Ecclesiastes 12:14 says, "For God will bring every deed into judgment, including every hidden thing, whether it is good or evil."

Hebrews 4:12,13 states —

> For the word of God is living and active. Sharper than any double-edged sword, it penetrates even to dividing soul and spirit, joints and marrow; it judges the thoughts and attitudes of the heart. Nothing in all creation is hidden from God's sight. Everything is uncovered and laid bare before the eyes of Him to whom we must give account.

Christ "will bring to light what is hidden in darkness and will expose the motives of men's hearts. At that time each will receive his praise from God" (I Corinthians 4:5). Revelation 22:12 reveals, "Behold, I am coming soon! My reward is with Me, and I will give to everyone according to what he has done." Matthew 19:30 indicates, "But many who are first will be last, and many who are last will be first."

James 3:1 cautions leaders —

> Not many of you should presume to be teachers, my brothers, because you know that we who teach will be judged more strictly.

I John 2:28 encourages us —

> And now, dear children, continue in Him, so

that when He appears we may be confident and unashamed before Him at His coming.

Called to Be Faithful, Not Successful

I attempt to live my life as one who must one day give an account to God for how I used the talents, finances, facilities, and staff He has entrusted to me.

Colossians 3:23,24 states —

> Whatever you do, work at it with all your heart, as working for the Lord, not for men, since you know that you will receive an inheritance from the Lord as a reward. It is the Lord Christ you are serving.

Remember, God looks at the motives of our hearts. He has not merely called us to be successful, but first and foremost, to be faithful. Revelation 2:10 says, "… Be faithful, even to the point of death, and I will give you the crown of life."

When we stand before the Lord, the only opinion that will really matter is His. I don't know about you, but when I see the Lord I want to hear Him say as He did in Matthew 25:23 —

> Well done, good and faithful servant! You have been faithful with a few things; I will put you in charge of many things. Come and share your master's happiness!

Our primary goal should not be to seek a large and successful ministry, but to seek His will and His glory and to be faithful to Him. The Lord desires to greatly use those who first seek His interests and not their own.

We should learn from the example of King Saul that not only will pride and disobedience destroy us, but when we see others prospering or other ministries or churches growing and accomplishing much for the Lord, we must not allow jealousy, envy, or bitterness to become rooted in our hearts.

When I see genuine ministries and churches proclaiming Scriptural truth and Biblical Christianity being blessed, I am overjoyed. I don't care if it is my ministry or another ministry, as long as the Lord's Kingdom is truly being advanced. I Corinthians 12:26 states, "... if one part is honored, every part rejoices with it."

Two Things That Will Destroy

When I first started this ministry, the Lord spoke to my heart that He would greatly use and bless me if I remained faithful. He warned that sin, especially pride or sexual immorality, would destroy my life and ministry, if I let either get a foothold.

As I spend time in prayer and fasting, I ask the Lord to search my heart and examine my motives. I ask Him to reveal, forgive, and remove any self-centeredness, self-motivation, and self-exaltation, and to help me be Christ-centered, Christ-motivated, and Christ-exalting. I also ask Him to not allow me to tolerate pride, haughtiness, bragging, and boasting, but by His Spirit to burn it out of my life and enable me to overcome it. I ask Him to never let me forget what I was before, where He brought me from, what He has done for me, and how He has humbled me when I became proud, so I will walk in humility and meekness before Him.

Honestly Examine Your Heart

Right now take time to honestly examine your heart. What are the motives for the things you do or the ministry you have? Is it merely for the praise of men and for your own exaltation, or is it truly for the glory of God? Is it to advance His Kingdom, or merely to build your own? Is what you do and say for popularity, convenience, and security, or is it in obedience to His Word and Spirit?

Make it a regular practice to get before the Lord

and evaluate your attitudes and motives. Allow Him to burn out any pride, haughtiness, bragging, boasting, rebellion, self-centeredness, and self-exaltation.

When you seek to walk in humility and meekness before the Lord, and the motivation and desire of your heart is to truly glorify Him, then you have laid an important foundation for a successful life and ministry. God will use you to fulfill the tremendous purpose and potential He has for you!

Live a Life of Integrity

Before I was a Christian, I had been a con, a liar and a thief. I had stolen and robbed and cheated many people. Even after giving my life to Christ, there were many things in my lifestyle to change — as the God of the Bible, through His Word and Spirit, began to transform my life.

God Sees Our Lack of Integrity

I hadn't been a Christian very long when I decided that rather than walk downtown to buy something I needed, I would take my father's worn-out 1966 Super Sport convertible, which at the time had neither license plate nor insurance. While backing out of a parking lot, I hit a parked car. After looking around and determining that no one had seen me, I took off. But someone had seen me — God.

Character is not what you do when people are watching. Character is what you do when no one else sees. It's just between you and God. As David points out, God sees and knows all about us —

O Lord, You have searched me and You know me. You know when I sit and when I rise; You perceive my thoughts from afar. You discern my going out and my lying down; You are familiar with all my ways. Before a word is on my tongue You know it completely, O Lord ....

Where can I go from Your Spirit? Where can I flee from Your presence? If I go up to the heavens, You are there; if I make my bed in the depths, You are there ....

If I say, "Surely the darkness will hide me and the light become night around me," even the darkness will not be dark to You; the night will shine like the day, for darkness is as light to You ....

Search me, O God, and know my heart; test me and know my anxious thoughts. See if there is any offensive way in me, and lead me in the way everlasting (Psalm 139:1-24).

Proverbs 5:21 reveals —

For a man's ways are in full view of the Lord, and He examines all his paths.

Another revealing account of my early Christian life illustrates how deception breeds more deception, and that once we begin to be deceitful and dishonest in one area of our life, it's like a cancer — it continues to grow and consume us. One week after my conversion, Karen and I decided to run away to West Virginia to get married. I was 18 and she was 17. Once the clerk at the courthouse verified our ages, she told us we needed to get blood tests and also get parental consent since we were underage.

After getting our blood tests in West Virginia, we went back to Pennsylvania where we filled out a marriage application form. The notary, who was a neighbor of mine, said we needed to have at least one of each of our parents sign in his presence. Knowing our parents would never sign, I told the notary that my mom was very sick at home in bed and unable to come to sign and that Karen's mother was also unable to do so. We forged our mothers' signatures and took the form back to the notary to be notarized.

Lack of Integrity Breeds Deceit

Once we forged the signatures we thought that was the end of it, but we were wrong. As the Scriptures illustrate in the lives of such important Biblical figures as Abraham, Isaac, and Jacob, deceit leads to deceit. Abraham deceived the Pharaoh in Egypt, and later King Abimelech, by claiming his beautiful wife Sarah was merely his sister (Genesis 12:10-20; 20:1-18). In turn, Abraham's son Isaac did the same thing by saying his wife Rebekah was his sister (Genesis 26:7-11). Then Isaac's son Jacob, coached by his mother Rebekah, deceived Isaac into blessing Jacob instead of Esau. Rebekah dressed Jacob to appear to be Esau. As a result, the first born's blessing and birthright that belonged to Esau was given to Jacob (Genesis 27:1-29). And on and on the deception went.

Jacob was deceived by his uncle Laban, who substituted Leah his oldest daughter for Rachel, the one Jacob loved, after he worked seven years for her (Genesis 29:13-30). Jacob's sons also deceived him by taking their brother Joseph's multicolored robe, dipping it in goat's blood and then showing it to their father, letting him think Joseph was killed by a wild animal, when in fact they sold him as a slave into Egypt (Genesis 37:21-36). For many years, until Joseph revealed himself to his brothers in Egypt and saved his family from starvation, they let their father Jacob be deceived.

Getting back to our story ... Karen and I returned to West Virginia with the appropriate paper work, but we were informed by the courthouse clerk that we needed both sets of parents' signatures. So we told her our parents were at a racetrack down the road and we would have them sign. Instead, we forged the signatures and returned the signed document to the clerk who said, "Okay, you can get married now."

Learning Integrity is a Process

So what happened to Abraham, Isaac, and Jacob? As Scripture informs us, God began to work in their hearts to the degree that they are presented in Hebrews chapter 11 as heroes of the faith. For example, Abraham became such a man of faith that he was willing to offer his son on the altar as a sacrifice before God. Jacob was humbled by God. He wrestled with an angel who touched his hip and caused him to walk with a limp the rest of his life, indicating to us that God will not let anyone get away with deceit and a lack of integrity. Joseph's brothers were changed men when he met them years later in Egypt, and they became heads of the tribes of Israel.

Years passed before Karen and I realized that the minister who married us never sent us a copy of our marriage license. We wondered whether he even recorded it at the courthouse, and if our marriage was legal since we forged the signatures. Not certain of the name of the city we were married in, and not wanting the hassle of tracking everything down, we forgot about it. But in February of 1994, while working on my records for an upcoming book entitled *The Impossible* and this *Integrity chapter*, I decided to get a copy of our marriage certificate — if one existed. By doing some research into our old scrapbooks, I discovered we were married in New Cumberland, West Virginia. I talked to the Hancock County clerk and told her I was compiling information for an upcoming article and book. She was most cooperative and even went to the courthouse basement to dig out the records from 1971. She graciously sent us a copy of our marriage certificate.

I told her that when we ran away to get married, I was a brand-new Christian, and we had forged our parents' signatures. She replied that regardless of that, the marriage was still legally binding, and many people had often lied about their ages and later wanted to change the records for Social Security reasons, etc. She said that now, if someone is under 21, both parents have to come in person to sign.

She was happy to hear that we got our start in West Virginia and were still married. She was excited to hear how God had worked in our lives and ministry. I sent her several of our ministry newsletters and a few of the books and pamphlets I had written.

God takes us where we are and works with us by the power of His Holy Spirit if we will allow Him free reign in our lives. Like our forefathers in the faith, Abraham, Isaac, and Jacob, God has brought us a long way.

Return Stolen Items

Before giving my life to Christ, I had stolen hundreds of dollars' worth of items. When I was a Christian for only a few months, God's Spirit began to deal with me, and I began to return things to the different stores and places from which I had stolen them. At first I took back the things I liked the least: the rock albums, the clothes, the jewelry, and the colognes. Then after a few more weeks, God's Spirit dealt with me again, and I looked for more things I had stolen. I returned a billy club, bayonet, and other weapons. Finally, a few weeks later, God's Spirit came heavily upon me to get rid of everything. I returned the weights, the remaining clothes, my favorite speed bag, and other things I knew I could never afford. But I had to obey.

Karen and I even took money to some of the stores where we could not return the items, because they were ruined or lost. The store clerks were bewildered. I told them, "Listen, I had stolen things before I was a Christian. Now I'm a believer in Jesus Christ. Please take the money." They thought we were crazy, but before my Lord I wanted to maintain my integrity.

We Rationalize "Little" Things

God had dealt with me as a new Christian about blatant thievery, deceit, and dishonesty, but I saw nothing wrong with the little things I still tried to justify. As human beings we try to make excuses to justify our behavior. You know the type of rationalizing — like what I once did: "They make me work extra hours at the window factory and don't pay me very good money, so it's no big deal if I take some nails. Besides, all the other Bible college students who work there are taking them, and they have been Christians much longer than me."

We also rationalized little things when I worked for a financial services company selling life insurance and financial investments with other Bible college students. Although we never outright lied, we led customers on by making our investments sound better than they actually were. Deceit can be a subtle thing.

Consumed by Fire

As I grew in the Lord, I began to learn the reality of Isaiah 33:14 -16. It refers to God as a consuming fire, and asks the question, "Who of us can dwell with the consuming fire?" The answer is, "He who walks righteously and speaks what is right, who rejects gain from extortion and keeps his hand from accepting bribes ...." God slowly burned deception and dishonesty out of me like fire purifies metal. I now strive in every way possible to live an upright and blameless life before the Lord and the world.

Integrity in "Little" Things

Some may think I go too far. For example, a lady once brought me a padlock to put on the gate of our ministry center's fence. After questioning her, I discovered that the lock had been taken from her husband's place of employment. She thought I was making a big deal out of it and claimed that other Christian leaders had accepted the locks. I said,

"Listen, even though it seems insignificant to you, if I keep this lock, I will be compromising my integrity before the God whom I seek to walk before with a pure heart, the God who has given me this land and this building, and who has blessed and greatly honored this ministry. I don't want to lose His presence or His blessing."

God is opposed to dishonesty in little things. No one will get away with making light of *little* acts of lying and deceit. The Bible says in Luke 16:10 —

> Whoever can be trusted with very little can also be trusted with much, and whoever is dishonest with very little will also be dishonest with much.

Matthew 25:21 confirms this truth —

> ... You have been faithful with a few things; I will put you in charge of many things ....

A Good Name Is Better Than Riches

Someone had donated several hundred dollars over the course of a year to our ministry, as well as to several other ministries. We found out later that the money had been embezzled from where this person worked. The owners of the company, needless to say, were upset. They wanted all the organizations who had received the embezzled monies to pay it back immediately.

Although we had no legal obligation to do so, and did not have the money to spare, we decided to comply with their request. To me our testimony was more important than money. Besides, it would help reduce the debt of the person who was accused of the embezzling.

We were the first ministry to pay back the money, and as a result, were spotlighted in the media. A lady who was impressed that we had agreed to pay back the money, gave us a check for the total amount. The company the money was embezzled from actually continued to occasionally support our ministry.

The Pain and Benefits of Integrity

What are the benefits of walking with integrity in the little things? Sometimes the value of choosing to live honestly is nothing more than a clear conscience and restful night of sleep. Other times you can actually see the hand of God bless in a material way.

For example, I had just finished doing two school assemblies in West Virginia. Traveling through the mountains of Virginia in our '85 Astro van to our next engagement in Baltimore, the van completely shut down. We had the van towed to a Chevy dealer, and it was discovered that because of an oil leak the engine was blown. An improperly tightened oil plug was the cause, which was an apparent act of negligence on the part of the place that last changed the oil. The cost to replace the engine was about $2,000 for a new one and $1,700 for a rebuilt one, so we wondered if the extended warranty would cover it since it was an oil leak. The service manager said that if we replaced the rubber oil plug with an original metal one that we would probably be covered by the warranty.

Here's where it hurts. I told him I was a Christian and would not do it. I also could have had the place that changed the oil pay for the expenses, but they had been donating their services for several years. We had the van towed back to Pennsylvania, where a local dealer put in a rebuilt engine for the discounted price of $1,400. Several people gave toward the cost, as the Lord provided all the money.

Not only were we able to be a good witness to all the people involved, we also saw the material blessing. The dealer who replaced the engine for us agreed to a unique deal. They bought a car that the ministry needed and would fit our budget and then traded us even, the van for that car. So not only had the Lord provided us with a van for the past three-and-a-half years, but as we traded the van in, He provided us with a car that was like brand-new without spending a cent. I believe that what made this all possible was our refusing to compromise on such a *little* thing as an oil plug.

$250 Money Order

One of countless more examples I could cite occurred when Karen received an order for two of my booklets from an ad in a magazine. However, she noticed the enclosed money order was for $250 instead of $2.50. With the volume of mail Karen has to deal with, she could have easily deposited it, not taking the time to check it out, thinking that maybe this person wanted to give an additional contribution as many do. But she felt it was a mistake. She notified our local post office, who then contacted the Florida post office which issued the money order. The clerk at that post office was greatly appreciative of our honesty, because she would have had to pay the difference of $247.50 out of her pocket.

Gimmickry and Merchandising the Gospel

Think about Paul's last words to the elders of Ephesus —

> You know how I lived the whole time I was with you, from the first day I came into the province of Asia. I have not coveted anyone's silver or gold or clothing. You yourselves know that these hands of mine have supplied my own needs and the needs of my companions. In everything I did, I showed you that by this kind of hard work we must help the weak, remembering the words the Lord Jesus Himself who said: "It is more blessed to give than to receive" (Acts 20:18, 33-35).

Consider Samuel's last words to Israel —

> Whose ox have I taken? Whose donkey have I taken? Whom have I cheated? Whom have I oppressed? From whose hand have I accepted a bribe to make me shut my eyes? If I have done any of these, I will make it right. "You have not cheated

or oppressed us," they replied. "You have not taken anything from anyone's hand" (I Samuel 12:3,4).

Then look at all the gimmickry going on today in many churches and ministries by Christian leaders. Many send out "personalized" computer letters causing naive people to think they are receiving a personal letter. Others use manipulation, coercion, or gimmicks to raise funds. They lie or exaggerate concerning what they are doing or how the money will be used.

Too many ministers are enriching themselves with great material possessions from those who give sacrificially. Some go so far as to suggest that donors give multiple tithes or take out a loan and send them the money. These religious shysters will mail out prayer cards and prayer cloths, promising to pray for healings and financial blessings if money is sent to them. They charge exorbitant fees to minister and for their products.

This is blatant merchandising of the Gospel. It's deceit and manipulation, and it's wrong.

In contrast, Paul stated in II Corinthians 2:17 —

> Unlike so many, we do not peddle the word of God for profit. On the contrary, in Christ we speak before God with sincerity, like men sent from God.

We had better heed the words in II Kings 5:16 that Elisha spoke to Naaman after the Lord used him to heal his leprosy and Naaman offered him a gift —

> "As surely as the Lord lives, whom I serve, I will not accept a thing." And even though Naaman urged him, he refused.

Then Elisha rebuked Gehazi, his greedy servant, who deceitfully hurried after Naaman to receive something for himself, as told in II Kings 5:26,27 —

> But Elisha said to him, "Was not my spirit with you when the man got down from his chariot to meet you? Is this the time to take money, or to

accept clothes, olive groves, vineyards, flocks, herds, or menservants and maidservants? Naaman's leprosy will cling to you and to your descendants forever." Then Gehazi went from Elisha's presence and he was leprous, as white as snow.

$10,000 Loan

We built our first ministry center on faith, and not a penny of interest was paid, nor was any money borrowed from a bank. When we were almost finished in March of 1982, I encouraged our staff and Board to pray, fast, and believe the Lord to provide $10,000 that month to meet some of the remaining expenses for building materials.

Shortly thereafter, a lady asked me if I would be offended if she offered to loan the ministry a large amount of money that we could pay back in three years without any interest. I asked how much she was talking about and she said, "as much as you need."

I reminded her that she could make a lot of interest by investing it, but she definitely felt the Lord wanted her to lend it to us. I told her I wouldn't even consider it unless she prayed about it for the next week. I said, "If in a week you change your mind, fine, but if not, then I will share it with my Board."

A week later she said she still felt the Lord would have her to do it. Although she would have lent us much more, because we had been asking the Lord for $10,000 that month, that is the amount I felt led to accept.

She met with our Board and they approved the agreement. The Lord blessed and we were able to pay her back ahead of schedule.

$1,000 Gift

Several years later, we felt led to build an addition — and to do so once again on faith and without paying any interest. It was the middle of March,

1986, when it hit us how crazy it seemed to begin building a large addition with our finances being so tight. But we knew the Lord wanted us to enter this venture, and He is always faithful to His Word.

It was about this time that a man stopped by the ministry center to see me. He gave me a check for $1,000 toward our new addition, informing me that he had been saving the money to repair his home. I said I didn't want to take his money, and that he should use it for his home. But he insisted, stating that he had spent much of the morning in prayer, and he felt strongly led by the Lord to give the $1,000, and his wife felt the same way.

Last Sin Mentioned in Revelation

Why is this chapter on deceit and dishonesty so crucial? In the last two chapters of Revelation, God strongly warns about lying and deceit. In fact, the very last sin mentioned in the Bible is lying (Revelation 22:15).

Perhaps one of the reasons God mentions lying as the last sin in the Bible is because it was Satan's lie that resulted in the fall of mankind (Genesis 3:1-5). We are not to be conformed to Satan's image, who is a liar and the father of lies (John 8:44), but we are to be conformed to the likeness of Jesus Christ (Romans 8:29) who walked in truth and integrity.

Revelation 21:8 indicates that "all liars will be in the fiery lake of burning sulfur." Revelation 21:27 reveals that no one who does what is "deceitful" will enter God's Holy City. Revelation 22:15 makes known that "everyone who loves and practices falsehood" will not be allowed to enter God's eternal Kingdom. In contrast, Revelation 22:14 God promises —

> Blessed are those who wash their robes, that they may have the right to the tree of life and may go through the gates into the city.

God has prepared the New Jerusalem for true

believers in Christ. The whole universe is at our disposal. We have all eternity to enjoy His blessings. If we have been faithful over small things, He will make us ruler over much.

The only way for us to enter the New Jerusalem to rule and reign with Christ for eternity, and to have everything He has prepared, is through faith in Jesus Christ. If you quit lying today, if you quit deceiving, if you quit stealing, if you quit all the things I'm talking about this day, and you do not put your trust in Jesus Christ for salvation, the Bible says your part will still be in the lake of fire.

But we who have been redeemed by Christ, whose names are written in the Lamb's Book of Life, must live like the One we claim to follow. We must continually allow God to crucify and burn out of us any deceit, exaggeration, falsehood, and lying, and instead strive to always be upright, honest, and truthful.

My Prayer

God is not only looking for men and women of courage, strength, and power who will stand up and impact this world for Christ, He is also looking for those who will not be compromised by dishonest gain, deception, lying lips, and falsehood. He's looking for men and women who will live a life of integrity before Him and this world.

That is why my prayer has been:

Lord, I am a person who was far from perfect and who made many mistakes. But at an early age in my walk with You, You began to burn deceit and dishonesty out of me, and by Your Word and Spirit You taught me to overcome that. I ask that You would help me to always walk uprightly before You; without exaggeration, without deceitful lips, without motivation for selfish gain. Help me to honor You in all things.

I pray that Your Spirit will speak to the heart of

each person reading this. Reveal any area of their life where they are allowing deceit, deception, exaggeration, lying lips, dishonest gain, or selfish motivation to control them or cause them to violate what Your Word strongly warns against. I ask that You would deal with them by Your Spirit so they would repent of it before You. Give them the assurance of Your forgiveness, and motivate them to walk in integrity. I ask this in Jesus' name. Amen.

Develop a Balanced Life

Luke 2:52 states, "And Jesus grew in wisdom and stature, and in favor with God and men." Jesus developed a balanced life.

Yet the truth is that many Christians are unbalanced. Either they only care about the spiritual and ignore the physical, or they place too much emphasis on the physical dimension and too little on the spiritual. As believers in Jesus, we should seek to glorify God with every aspect of our lives.

We must be careful that we do not keep in shape and seek to have a healthy body merely because it is the current trend, or because we want to impress everyone with our great physiques. We should do it so we can truly glorify God with every aspect of our lives. It's great if we can add ten or fifteen years to our life spans with good, healthful living, but it is more important that we come to know the source of abundant and eternal life, Jesus Christ. He said, "I have come that they may have life, and have it to the full" (John 10:10).

As I read in Scripture concerning God's precise requirements for construction and care for the tabernacle and temple in the Old Testament, I realize the tremendous responsibility to take care of my body, the temple of the Holy Spirit (1 Corinthians 6:19,20).

In order to achieve our maximum potential in Christ we must develop balanced lives. This includes taking care of our bodies (which are the temples of the Holy Spirit) and offering them to God as "living sacrifices" (Romans 12:1). It also consists of our minds being filled and renewed by God's Word and living according to its truth (Romans 12:2). This results in mental and emotional health and in having "the mind of Christ" (I Corinthians 2:16).

Above all, we must grow spiritually by living under His Lordship and seeking to be conformed to His image (Romans 8:29). When the world sees how our faith in Christ positively impacts every aspect of our lives — physically, mentally/emotionally, and spiritually — many will want to know the Christ we serve. We will also have increased energy and vitality for accomplishing the Lord's will.

On my *Steps To Optimum Health* poster, I list the following to help remind me how to live a balanced life:

- Honor the Lord in all things
- Read the Word and pray daily
- Watch and read only that which is truly profitable
- Have a positive mental attitude
- Walk in the Lord's peace and rest in Him
- Get proper sleep, rest, and relaxation
- Get regular exercise
- Replace junk food with nutritious food
- Eat mostly fresh fruits and vegetables, raw nuts and seeds, and natural whole-grain breads and cereals

- Chew food thoroughly to aid proper digestion, assimilation, and elimination
- Drink plenty of pure water and fruit and vegetable juices
- Use wisdom to prevent careless accidents and injuries
- Avoid excessive sun exposure and needless pollutants

Self-Control —
the Essence of Strength

From traveling and ministering throughout the U.S. and abroad and receiving thousands of letters from around the world, I have discovered that one of the biggest problems Christian adults and teens (as well as non-Christians) face is a lack of discipline and self-control. Almost all the troubles people get into and the problems they encounter, (whether it's related to drugs or alcohol; lust and sexual immorality which lead to broken relationships, unwanted pregnancies, venereal disease, or AIDS; overeating, stealing, lying, or gossiping; jealousy, bitterness, revenge, outbursts of anger, or violence) could possibly have been avoided if they only had exercised more discipline and self-control.

As stated previously, when I first started this ministry the Lord spoke to my heart that He would greatly use and bless me if I remained faithful. He warned that sin, especially sexual immorality or pride, would destroy my life and ministry, if I let either get a foothold. Therefore, whenever I spend time in prayer and fasting, I ask the Lord to help me by His Spirit to root out, overcome, and burn out of my life any sin, disobedience, immorality, and lust. I pray that by His Spirit, He will enable me to walk in obedience, control, and discipline, and to desire Him more than anything or anyone else — to have a hunger and thirst and passion for Him!

I Was Out of Control

Before coming to Christ, I was out of control in almost every area of my life. I couldn't control my stealing. I would walk into a store and walk out with almost anything I wanted. I stole so much it became second nature. I'd steal without hesitation and sometimes without even realizing I was doing it. Even as a new Christian, when I was in a store or situation that was very similar to something I was in before I was a Christian, my mind would flash back, and I'd still feel guilty and strange as if I was being watched because someone thought I was trying to steal something.

Eating was another area in which I was out of control. As a kid I was a junk food addict. I would steal money from my dad and oldest brother to buy candy bars and all kinds of junk food. I craved chocolate, sugar, salt, and greasy foods. One time I stole $20 from my oldest brother and took a neighbor girl to a nearby convenience store. I bought her milk shakes, candy bars, and other items. When I paid with a $20 bill, they called my parents. My brother came to get me, and smacked me all the way home for stealing from him.

When my friends and I became teens, we frequently slept out under the stars. We would load up on junk food to eat throughout the night. Usually I would buy a couple quarts of soda pop or a half gallon of chocolate milk, along with cupcakes, donuts, candy bars, and potato chips. My friend's girlfriend worked at a candy store. On Sunday afternoons she would be working alone, so we came in to eat anything we wanted, and also took bags of candy home. As a child, almost all my baby teeth were rotten, and as a teen I had teeth pulled and many fillings due to all the sugar-laden foods I had consumed.

Drinking was also a problem for me. I couldn't control my use of alcohol. I lived to get high on weekends and holidays. One night I was so drunk I almost fell through a large storefront window in my hometown. On numerous occasions I was in wrecks and near tragedies because of being out of control due to the influence of alcohol.

I loved gambling so much that it too began to control me. For weeks at a time my friends and I would go on gambling sprees, during which my whole life would revolve around gambling. We would play cards all night and even developed an intricate cheating system by using our eyes. This system won us a lot of money, but it eventually almost got us "lynched." Once at a local bazaar, I convinced the dealer in a poker booth to give me extra cards, with the promise that afterwards I would split the profits with him. He did, but I took off and never gave him anything.

My mouth was out of control. If I wasn't lying, I was telling someone off. I couldn't control my lying. I lied so well, I convinced myself. My mouth was always getting me in trouble. I often had older guys waiting for me after school or looking for me or sending someone else after me because of something smart I said to them or something offensive I said to their girlfriend.

Controlled by lust, I was compulsively looking for more excitement and pleasure. In the process, I used and abused a lot of people.

Addicted to adrenaline, I would try every thrill imaginable to experience a temporary high, like the time I drove down the highway at 115 mph in my dad's convertible, thinking I was *god*, and that if I hit something I would not be killed. The fastest I ever went down a highway was 135 mph in my friend's car. I loved the sensation of speed and thrived on jumping trains and bumper dragging cars in the snow. I jumped off train trestles into the the waters of the dam even though I was afraid of heights. I forced myself to do it because of peer pressure and a desire for another thrill. Any adventurous activity became a passion.

My cheating was uncontrollable. I cheated or charmed my way through much of high school, and I thought I got away with it. Answers would be written up and down my arms, hidden under my desk, on my belt, and in my socks. I would sweet-talk girls to do assignments for me and pay or threaten guys to do them. But guess what? The only one I cheated was myself!

I expected to spend my life lifting weights and loafing on some secluded island beach somewhere. You could not have convinced me back then that God would one day change my life and call me into the ministry, that I would go to Bible college, and that I would need to apply what I learned in high school: English to write books, science and history for the research I would do, geography for the traveling I would be doing throughout the world to minister, math and algebra to understand finances, or languages when I went on missionary outreaches to foreign lands. At school, the only areas in which I applied myself were physical education and lunch.

When I went to Bible college, I had to spend time looking up words in the dictionary for spelling and meanings. It was much more difficult for me than most of the other students, because I had to learn what I missed in high school, as well as try to keep up with the information the Bible college instructors were teaching us. This difficulty was the result of the wasted high school years when I thought I was getting away with my cheating.

An additional problem was in the area of finances. When my wife and I ran away and got married as teenagers, although we were poor, we eventually followed the traditional American lifestyle of charge cards and loans. Before long we were over our heads in debt.

The Lord dealt with us, and we got rid of our credit cards and refused to take out any more interest loans. Eventually we did get more credit cards, but we pay them off each month so as not to incur any interest. We have applied the lessons we learned regarding finances to our ministry. That is one reason why it has operated so effectively on limited funds, and why we live better and happier than most people who have much more money but are deeply in debt.

I know what it means to be out of control. If God could bring my life under control, He can bring anyone's life under control.

The Scars Remain

There is another aspect to being out of control, and that is paying the consequences of wrong choices. As a result of my foolish, rebellious, out-of-control behavior, I'm paying the price with injuries from head to toe, because I (or someone near me) was out of control. The list of past injuries is long, and includes hyperextended and dislocated joints, broken bones, chipped teeth, scars, and tissue damage.

Once I was speaking and doing a demonstration at a youth camp. When I finished, a big burly guy in his 30's came over to me, moving slowly. He told me he had a bad back and arthritis in his hands. I said,

"I bet you loved to fight and busted a lot of heads when you were young." He asked, "How do you know?" I replied, "Because I recognize the consequences that occur because of that kind of lifestyle. I know the arthritis in your hands is from busting heads, and the bad back is a result of getting slammed to the ground."

The Bible says in Galatians 6:7,8 —

> Do not be deceived: God cannot be mocked. A man reaps what he sows. The one who sows to please his sinful nature, from that nature will reap destruction; the one who sows to please the Spirit, from the Spirit will reap eternal life.

I am a good illustration, for I am suffering many consequences from the foolish things I did before committing my life to Christ. I am not only trying to reverse some of those consequences through healthy living, but I am also letting people know that the Bible is true — you do reap what you sow.

Ecclesiastes 11:9 and 12:1 cautions us concerning how we live during our youth —

> Be happy, young man, while you are young, and let your heart give you joy in the days of your youth. Follow the ways of your heart and whatever your eyes see, but know that for all these things God will bring you to judgment. Remember your Creator in the days of your youth, before the days of trouble come and the years approach when you will say, "I find no pleasure in them."

Ecclesiastes 12:13,14 wisely concludes —

> Now all has been heard; here is the conclusion of the matter: Fear God and keep His commandments, for this is the whole duty of man. For God will bring every deed into judgment, including every hidden thing, whether it is good or evil.

You're free to make almost any choice you want. You can involve yourself in any kind of lifestyle you desire, but it's like being on a high roof. You can jump off if you want. You are free to make that decision. Once you jump off, however, you are no longer free. You are now a slave to the law of gravity which will splatter you on the ground below.

While you do have freedom to choose to get involved in drugs, alcohol, immorality, gambling, stealing, lying, fighting, vandalism, gossiping, gluttony, or other destructive behavior, the consequences will one day catch up to you. I've seen it 100% of the time. Maybe not overnight, but eventually you will reap what you sow; physically, mentally/emotionally, and spiritually. So, use wisdom deciding in what you participate.

God will forgive, but the scars and consequences often remain. For example, if a drunken driver kills a little child, God will forgive him if he asks, but he'll live with that memory for the rest of his life. That's why it is so important to develop self-control now!

Weakness is Lacking Self-Control

Proverbs 25:28 states —

Like a city whose walls are broken down is a man who lacks self-control.

In Biblical days cities often had walls built around them, which made them strong and easy to defend fortresses. If the walls were broken down, the people were vulnerable and defenseless against the enemies' attacks. So God is saying, "If you have self-control, it's like having a wall around the city — you're strong. However, a person without self-control is weak, defenseless, and vulnerable."

Alexander the Great was a powerful man who conquered and controlled most of the known world. His empire extended from Greece to India, but he could not conquer his lusts. He died at age 33 after taking ill following a prolonged banquet and drinking bout. Is that real control? Is that strength? Is that what you want in your life?

Consider many of the rock stars, movie actors, and great athletes who are often idolized. They flaunt their out-of-control and rebellious lifestyles. Many covet their fame, money, and power. But the outcome of their lives is often tragedy. That's not the end result that God desires for you.

Proverbs 16:32 says —

He who is slow to anger is better than the mighty, and he who rules his spirit, than he who captures a city (NAS).

You can go out and conquer a city — even conquer the world — but if you cannot tame your spirit, you have not achieved the strength that God wants you to have. Controlling your very spirit, temper, desires, thoughts, and behavior, is better than conquering other people or achieving great accomplishments.

I know those who can do phenomenal, almost superhuman, feats. Yet many of those same people can't control their tongues or tempers. They are unable to control their lust, jealousy, hatred, bitterness, worry, or fear. That is weakness, not strength. Is there any real benefit in the ability to do phenomenal feats when the rest of a person's life is out of control? Far more important than external displays of power is the inner molding of our character, attitudes, and spirit.

The Essence of Strength is Self-Control

The world's view of strength is distorted. It equates strength with fighting better, drinking more alcohol, jumping from bed to bed, acting wild and crazy, robbing and vandalizing. But that's a lie. I know because I lived that lie. If you think that is strength, then you are being deceived. I have told young people and adults, including many military, martial artists, weight lifters, gang members, and prisoners throughout the U.S. and world that anyone can live a life out of control. I can teach anyone to fight, rob and steal, vandalize, swear, smoke, drink, and do drugs. Any wimp can do that. But it takes true courage, strength, and self-control to resist the peer pressure and live for Christ. Let's expose the lie that the world has been telling us about what is cool and what is strength.

Before I stopped doing demonstrations, I illustrated this point in school assemblies and detention centers by doing two back kicks. First, I would demonstrate a kick to the chest with no control, knocking my assistant back. "Anyone can do that," I'd say. "It's very easy to kick with no control."

Once I was speaking at a high school assembly to several hundred juniors and seniors in a cafeteria setting. They were seated at tables in groups of eight all around the stage area. The assistant I was using was a big guy who played basketball for one of the Penn State branches. I did the "out-of-control kick," but I must have kicked him harder than he expected and he went flying back about six feet and hit an easel. The easel flipped in the air as it flew off the stage, crashing in the middle of a table of students, and breaking apart. For the rest of that assembly not one student in the audience talked or moved, but paid close attention.

The second kick was also at full speed, but I would stop my foot within a fraction of an inch of my assistant's face, or lightly touch his face with the bottom of my foot. I would also do about 15 hand techniques at full speed, within a fraction of an inch of my assistant's face. Because I used control, I never touched him. "To have control," I would explain, "requires far more strength and ability."

Another time I was speaking on peer pressure and self-control at a youth detention center. About halfway through I made the mistake of mentioning that I often demonstrate two kicks, but I couldn't that night because I had slippery boots on (I had no intention of doing the kicks).

They didn't want to hear that. They said, "No! we want to see it!" So I said, "Okay, who wants to volunteer?" Nobody moved. Finally, after some prompting by his peers, a big guy called Samson agreed and came down front with me.

All of a sudden over 100 youth rushed to the front and surrounded us to watch, as if it were going to be an actual fight. I was thinking, "Lord, what did I get myself into? If I slip and hit this guy in the chin, it could turn into a riot. If I kick too far away from his chin to avoid slipping in these boots and hitting him, it's going to look so unimpressive that I'll lose the impact I'm having. You've got to help me." Thank the Lord, it went perfectly. I came within a fraction of an inch of his face at full speed. As a result, they all went back to their seats and listened intently, and over twenty of them came forward during the altar call.

It is the controlled person who is the powerful person. In the Greek, "without self-control" means powerless or without strength — therefore, the Biblical inference is: a person without self-control is weak, and a person with self-control is strong.

Before I became a Christian, I thought Christians were weak. That's one reason why I didn't want to give my life to Christ. I later discovered it takes more strength to live for Jesus Christ than for any other lifestyle.

I equated strength with how much you could bench press, how many people you could beat up, or how much you could drink. I soon realized that is not the essence of true strength. Physical strength does not impress me now as much as inner strength. Being able to chug a six-pack of beer, bench press 400 pounds, or defeat ten others at the same time is not as powerful as having self-control. There is a power greater than physical strength, and that is the inner strength and control that comes through the transforming power of God's Spirit.

Even after I became a Christian, I had an extensive, intensive, and rigorous weightlifting and martial arts training program before God led me out. In three hours a week, I would accomplish more and achieve a higher level of conditioning and efficiency than most people did with ten hours a week. But God began to deal with me about what constitutes real strength. I still exercise to keep in shape, but I have discontinued my extensive training. I put down my desire for physical strength and power for something far more important — inner strength, character, and spiritual power.

How to Develop Self-Control

Some of these illustrations show the consequences of not having self-control and the great benefits from having it. I could have shared many more, but hopefully I have given enough to motivate you to desire the tremendous benefits that having self-control will bring. So how do you develop self-control? I am going to share some practical, yet crucial, principles from God's Word concerning how you can begin to develop discipline and self-control over every aspect of your life.

Many have made mistakes from being out of control in some area of their lives, but no matter what you've done, there is hope. As Jesus said to the woman caught in adultery, "Neither do I condemn you. Go now and leave your life of sin" (John 8:11). Written to believers, I John 1:9 states —

> If we confess our sins, He is faithful and just and will forgive us our sins and purify us from all unrighteousness.

You have to assume responsibility for your behavior. Many people like to blame their problems on their parents, their environment, peer pressure, God, or Satan. That should not be surprising, for from the beginning of human history, we have been blaming others. When God confronted Adam after he ate the forbidden fruit, Adam blamed Eve and said, "It's the woman you gave me, God." Eve said, "It's the serpent." So too, many Christians today attribute their out-of-control behavior to Satan or someone or something other than themselves. If we are going to change, we must assume responsibility for our own behavior and quit blaming others.

When my son was just a child, he began to stick out his tongue while I was teaching him things such as self-defense, hitting the speed bag, and gymnastics. I warned him by saying, "B.J., don't do that because you will develop a habit you can't break." He would answer, "Come on, Dad, no problem." He thought it was cute, so he kept doing it.

When he was a little older and was playing soccer in an older kids' league or basketball at school, he often had his tongue hanging out. He'd be dribbling down the field or basketball court, and if he wasn't thinking about it, his tongue would be out. I said, "See how you developed a habit you can't stop?" He agreed to cooperate with me in overcoming it, so every time I saw it out, I kept saying, "B.J., get it in." Finally after months of reminding him, he overcame that habit.

I have cautioned many people who were abusing themselves physically by over consumption of junk food and other unhealthy practices. Most smiled at me and said, "No problem. It's not hurting me." I usually responded, "You can either choose to discipline yourself now or one day you will be forced to." Sure enough, because of health problems, many of these people have already been forced by doctors to change their diets and lifestyles. For some it was too late, and contributed to their untimely deaths.

You Have to Be Motivated

I prayed many times to overcome several sins from my past that controlled me. However, I was continually defeated because I was not really motivated. But the Lord knows how to motivate. He convinced me that my old lifestyle led to death and destruction. That motivated me to take steps to bring my life under control.

When I really wanted to be set free, and I truly repented before the Lord, He intervened and gave me the wisdom and power of His Spirit to walk in victory according to the principles of His Word.

Flee Youthful Lusts

Follow the advice of II Timothy 2:22, "Flee also youthful lusts (KJV)." Avoid movies, music, magazines, places, and people that entice you to sin. Before you let the situation get out of control — STOP! Think about the consequences. Depend on the Spirit of God to give you the wisdom and self-control to resist the temptation and to even flee the scene if necessary (Genesis 39:7-12).

When I taught self-defense clinics, I demonstrated how to avoid potential confrontations and how to deal with attack situations. "But the most important principle," I would tell the group, "is to use wisdom in avoiding places, people, and situations in which you know a confrontation or an attack is likely to occur." Likewise, to overcome temptation that controls you, avoid places, people, and situations that would entice you into sin and into compromising circumstances. I Thessalonians 5:22 wisely admonishes us to "Abstain from all appearance of evil" (KJV).

As a new Christian I used to think, "Lord, I'm going to put myself in the midst of every temptation so I can prove how powerful You are in enabling me to overcome them." I wondered why I was often being defeated. The Lord made me mindful of when the children of Israel entered and conquered the promised land. God told them to destroy all the idols and high places, and often to either kill all the men, women, and children or to drive them out (Exodus 34:11-13; Deuteronomy 7:1-5).

At first I thought this was cruel. I thought it revealed a weakness in Him — that He was unable to preserve His people in the midst of temptation. But the Lord knows the attraction and enticement of sin. He gives us wisdom to *avoid* temptation before it ensnares, enslaves, and destroys us — just as it did to Israel on numerous occasions when they violated God's commands.

Jesus knew how important it is to deal with and remove our source of temptation. He said in Matthew 18:8,9 —

> If your hand or your foot causes you to sin, cut it off and throw it away. It is better for you to enter life maimed or crippled than to have two hands or two feet and be thrown into eternal fire. And if your eye causes you to sin, gouge it out and throw it away. It is better for you to enter life with one eye than to have two eyes and be thrown into the fire of hell.

Jesus did not mean for you to do this literally. If that were so, the disciples and New Testament believers would all have been maimed and crippled. Rather, He wanted to emphasize the importance of using wisdom in removing and avoiding sources of temptation.

Stand faithfully on I Corinthians 10:13 which promises —

> No temptation has seized you except what is common to man. And God is faithful; He will not let you be tempted beyond what you can bear. But when you are tempted, He will also provide a way out so that you can stand up under it.

Do not purposely place yourself in a tempting situation and expect this principle to come to your rescue — that's flirting with failure and tempting God.

When you sin, quickly go before the Lord and confess your sin, realizing that He is now our great High Priest as shown in Hebrews 4:14-16 —

> Therefore, since we have a great high priest who has gone through the heavens, Jesus the Son of God, let us hold firmly to the faith we profess. For we do not have a high priest who is unable to sympathize with our weaknesses, but we have one who has been tempted in every way, just as we are — yet was without sin. Let us then approach the throne of grace with confidence, so that we may receive mercy and find grace to help us in our time of need.

One Area Affects All

One reason I fast, exercise, abstain from junk food, and limit my television viewing to that which is profitable is to help me develop self-control. I have learned that by being disciplined in these areas it makes it much easier for me to stay disciplined in other areas of my life as well. When I begin to let even one aspect of my life get out of control, it seems before I know it, many other areas also become undisciplined, like a domino effect.

Mental Discipline

If you want to change your behavior, you have to change your thought life. Mental discipline is crucial. If you want to control your words and actions, learn to control your thoughts and attitude.

Coaches tell players, "You give up first in your mind, then your body quits." When I was totally exhausted from working out on the trampoline, my gymnastic instructor would say, "You're not really tired. You can keep going. It's all in your head." I would think, "That's easy for you to say. I can't; I'm going to die." Then some girls would walk into the gym, and I would quickly revive. He was right, it was all in my mind.

For many years I was involved in gymnastics. I practiced doing back flips on the trampoline, on the mats, and in the grass. We would have an annual Super Circus to showcase our abilities. One of the performances I did was inherited from one of my older brothers. I would get in the middle of the trampoline with a blue cloth bag over my head and body, down to about my knees. There would also be a guy on each corner of the trampoline twirling a long rope around the middle of the trampoline. As they would twirl the rope around me, I would do back flips — about 20 of them in a row — while the bag was over my head and body.

As a young teenager, I did so many back flips during my gymnastics career, that something must have short-circuited in my brain. I would get on a trampoline, and instead of bouncing three times to get my height before doing the back flip, after only one bounce (and sometimes before I could even bounce), without thinking, I would do a back flip. I'd sometimes end up in the springs or on the floor. It got so bad that sometimes I'd be walking along in the yard and all of a sudden I'd do a back flip or a back handspring. I couldn't overcome that, and for a long time it controlled me. For years, before I became a Christian, I was afraid to get back on a trampoline.

Then I gave my life to Christ and He called me into the ministry. A local high school donated a trampoline to our ministry. Fifteen years had gone by, but that vivid memory returned. As I got on that trampoline I said, "God, Your Word says, 'I can do everything through Him who gives me strength' " (Philippians 4:13). I began to bounce slowly as I quoted that Scripture in my mind and told myself I could do it, refusing to be controlled by that fear.

I was soon able to do some of my old tricks and play trampoline basketball. I still have to be careful and keep my mind focused, but I have overcome this controlling fear by trusting the Lord and developing mental discipline.

Whether you're at work, on vacation, watching TV, driving down the road, walking at the mall, or even sitting in the pew, there are constant sources of temptation. We're all exposed! Billboards, advertisements, magazines, books, TV, music, and scantily clad people constantly stimulate the mind into lustful thoughts and lure us with temptations of pride, greed, and self-indulgence. It's only by the grace of God anyone survives unscathed in this decadent society.

Everyone has tempting thoughts, but you can control what you do with them. Your thoughts and temptations are not sin, unless you dwell on them or give in to them, What you do with those thoughts and with those temptations determines whether it is merely a temptation or actual sin.

In Matthew 15:19, Christ reveals that sin begins in the heart. He states: "For out of the heart come evil thoughts, murder, adultery, sexual immorality ...." Sin first begins in our hearts and minds. Therefore, if we are going to overcome the temptations we daily face, we must effectively eradicate these thoughts before they can control and enslave us.

What you program into your mind will eventually manifest in your thoughts, attitudes, words, and behavior. Your thoughts lead to attitudes. Your thoughts and attitudes produce an emotional response. Your thoughts, attitudes, and emotions lead to actions. Your actions lead to habits and patterns. Your habits and patterns lead to a lifestyle.

Your lifestyle effects your destiny.

That's why God puts so much emphasis on the heart and the inward man. He knows that if you are going to gain victory over your behavior and actions, you must control your thoughts and attitudes.

If you fill your mind with jealousy, you'll eventually end up with bitterness and gossiping. If you fill your mind with hatred and revenge, you'll end up verbally and/or physically abusing people. If you fill your mind with lustful thoughts and sex-oriented movies, books, and music, your involvement in sexual immorality is inevitable.

You may say, "My thoughts and attitudes don't affect me." Suppose a bear would come charging right at you. Because of the emotion of fear, numerous changes would occur immediately within your body: your pulse rate would increase; your breathing would become more rapid; adrenaline would flood your bloodstream; your pupils would become larger, enabling you to see better; your hearing would become more acute; your muscles would tense; and your blood pressure would rise.

All this and more would occur as your body prepares to defend itself or to run away. It is known as the fight-or-flight syndrome which occurs instantaneously when we encounter real or imaginary danger. Even if it really wasn't a bear, and you only thought it was, your emotional response of fear would still automatically cause these physical reactions.

The psyche or mind can produce varied effects in the body or soma; thus the term, psychosomatic. Our emotions and our thoughts do affect our behavior and our lifestyle.

If you fill your body with junk food, you will eventually develop a junky body. If you fill your mind with garbage, you will eventually develop a garbage thought life, mental attitude, and lifestyle. It's inevitable; it's just a matter of time. What we watch, read, and listen to does affect us.

I well remember how rock music affected my friends and me as teenagers. We used to start fights and act wild and crazy when certain songs came on. I wrecked several cars because certain songs motivated me to drive even faster and more recklessly than usual. I actually decided to hitchhike across the country, mainly because two popular songs of that time made it sound so exciting. I later discovered why the main rock group I liked had influenced me so much toward fighting and rebellious behavior. They were deeply involved in the occult.

It is not surprising that so many people have lustful thoughts and sexual problems. No wonder so many can't control their tongues, tempers, or appetites, or are controlled by worry, fear, jealousy, and bitterness. Their minds are programmed with degenerate materials.

The Lord has taught me that I must not tolerate certain thoughts. Thoughts of lust, worry, fear, jealousy, anger, revenge, pride, and greed that come into my mind are intruders that will destroy me. God says, "Resist them!" Fight against them as though you were fighting against an intruder in your house who was attempting to rape and kill your family. In such a situation I am sure you would stand and fight, and endure until every ounce of strength was gone.

Those thoughts of jealousy, bitterness, lust, or pride are intruders in your mind that will eventually destroy you if allowed to stay. You must say, "I will not tolerate these thoughts. I choose right now by an act of my will to resist them. I will not let jealousy, bitterness, fear, worry, anger, pride, and greed control me. I choose to show love and forgiveness, to walk in courage, faith, and meekness."

We must persistently say, "No!" to our temptations. James 4:7 says, "Submit yourselves, then, to God. Resist the devil, and he will flee from you."

Titus 2:11-13 says —

For the grace of God that brings salvation has appeared to all men. It teaches us to say 'No' to ungodliness and worldly passions, and to live self-controlled, upright and godly lives in this present age, while we wait for the blessed hope — the glorious appearing of our great God and Savior, Jesus Christ.

II Corinthians 7:1 says —

Since we have these promises, dear friends, let us purify ourselves from everything that contaminates body and spirit, perfecting holiness out of reverence for God.

We must develop discipline as the following Scriptures indicate.

II Corinthians 10:5 encourages us to "take captive every thought to make it obedient to Christ."

Romans 12:2 says —

Do not conform any longer to the pattern of this world, but be transformed by the renewing of your mind. Then you will be able to test and approve what God's will is — His good, pleasing and perfect will.

Psalm 119:9,11 asks, and then answers a very relevant question —

How can a young man keep his way pure? By living according to Your word. I have hidden Your word in my heart that I might not sin against You.

Philippians 4:8 tells us —

Finally, brothers, whatever is true, whatever is noble, whatever is right, whatever is pure, whatever is lovely, whatever is admirable — if anything is excellent or praiseworthy — think about such things.

Most Christians think all they have to do is avoid watching, reading, or listening to things that are bad for them. Scripture is telling us to not only do that, but to also watch, read, listen to, and associate with that which will be a positive influence in our lives and conform us to the likeness of Jesus Christ (Romans 8:29).

The Discipline of Daniel

Satan is in rebellion against the Lord, and wants to enslave and destroy you because you are a creation of God.

I Thessalonians 5:23 says —

> May God Himself, the God of peace, sanctify you through and through. May your whole spirit, soul and body be kept blameless at the coming of our Lord Jesus Christ.

God tells us that our bodies are the temples of the Holy Spirit. Satan wants to destroy our temples and mock God through tempting us to live a self-gratifying and self-destructive lifestyle.

God tells us the mind is a spiritual battleground and that we need to renew it and keep it on guard. Satan, on the other hand, wants it filled with garbage and put in a passive, neutral, non-resistant mental state.

God tells us our spirit is made in His image and that we are to be conformed to the image of Christ. Satan seeks to make us spiritual prostitutes by making someone or something else *god* in our lives and conforming us to his image of pride and rebellion against our Creator.

In that way Satan can say, "Look at your creation, God. See what they're doing to themselves. They are prostituting and destroying their bodies, minds, and spirits." Thereby, Satan, though far inferior to God in power and who cannot contend with Him, in some twisted and perverted way gets a sense of pleasure.

Daniel lived in a pagan, idolatrous, occultic, and self-gratifying environment, yet he stayed true to the God of the Bible. At times, his peers thought he was operating in the same powers they were, but Daniel walked in obedience, control, and discipline as he maintained his commitment to God.

Daniel made a decision not to defile himself with the king's choice food or wine (Daniel 1:8). He had physical discipline and self-control. He also did not fill his mind with or rely on sorcery and occultism (Daniel 2). He had mental discipline. Finally, he made a commitment to pray three times a day — even though it could cost him his life (Daniel 6). He had spiritual discipline.

God greatly blessed Daniel because of the obedience resulting from his physical, mental, and spiritual discipline. He was healthier than those who ate the king's choice food. When the magicians, conjurers, and sorcerers could not tell Nebuchadnezzar his dream or the interpretation, Daniel could. And God protected Daniel from certain death in the lions' den and greatly exalted him.

Live by the Spirit

We have freedom in Christ. However, if something controls you, you no longer have liberty, but enslavement. God wants you free.

The choice is yours — will you be controlled by the lusts of the flesh that eventually lead to destruction, death, and eternal separation from God, or will you be transformed by the Spirit of Christ, the fruit of which leads to tremendous victory, blessing, peace, and joy?

Galatians 5:16-25 states —

> So I say, live by the Spirit, and you will not gratify the desires of the sinful nature. For the

sinful nature desires what is contrary to the Spirit, and the Spirit what is contrary to the sinful nature. They are in conflict with each other, so that you do not do what you want. But if you are led by the Spirit, you are not under law.

The acts of the sinful nature are obvious: sexual immorality, impurity and debauchery; idolatry and witchcraft; hatred, discord, jealousy, fits of rage, selfish ambition, dissensions, factions and envy; drunkenness, orgies, and the like. I warn you, as I did before, that those who live like this will not inherit the kingdom of God.

But the fruit of the Spirit is love, joy, peace, patience, kindness, goodness, faithfulness, gentleness and self-control. Against such things there is no law. Those who belong to Christ Jesus have crucified the sinful nature with it's passions and desires. Since we live by the Spirit, let us keep in step with [walk in] the Spirit.

Galatians 5:22,23 reveals that self-control is a fruit of the Spirit, not of will power. If you try to develop self-control merely with your own strength and self-effort, you will be continually frustrated. You need God's Spirit to help bring your life under control. He will enable you to apply the Biblical principles necessary for developing self-control.

I tried to quit stealing. I tried to quit drinking. I tried to live by the Ten Commandments. But I was continually defeated. I was out of control. Although I could gain control for a few days or a few weeks at a time, it didn't last.

When I surrendered my will to Christ, He changed my life. As I sought the Lord with all my heart through studying His Word, prayer, and fasting, His Spirit continued transforming and empowering me. I was able through Him to develop the fruit of self-control.

The closer we draw to the Lord, by getting into His Word and allowing His Spirit to work in our lives, the more we will be conformed to His likeness, and the more we will manifest the fruit of His Spirit in our lives and walk in victory over that which controls us.

Controlled by Nothing but the Lord

Paul said in I Corinthians 6:12 —

All things are lawful for me, but not all things are profitable. All things are lawful for me, but I will not be mastered [or controlled] by anything (NAS).

I don't know about you, but I do not want to be controlled by my temper or my tongue. I do not want to be consumed with lust, greed, or fear. I do not want to be a slave to destructive habits such as drugs, alcohol, or stealing. I do not want to be victimized by peer pressure. I do not want to be mastered by sinful thoughts, attitudes, emotions, or actions. I only want to be controlled by my Lord. I want to bring every area of my life under His control and walk in His wisdom, strength, and empowerment.

It Takes Time

People often say to me, "Bill, I want you to pray for me. I want self-control from God and I want it now!" I wish I could lay hands on you and zap you so you would have all your problems removed and have instant self-control over every area of your life, but that's not the way it works. It took me years to obtain the self-control I have developed from walking with the Lord and applying the truth of His Word.

Once my younger brother and I were out playing football in the front yard when he was a teen. He had his shirt off and was trying to impress those walking or driving by our house. He was throwing the football as hard as he could. In between throws he was watching to make sure someone was watching him. I said, "Let's throw with the opposite hand." This time he looked around to make sure no one was watching because he threw like a sissy. But guess what, as we kept doing it over and over, we eventually got pretty good at it.

It takes time to develop self-control and discipline and to overcome old habits. If you persistently apply the principles I have been sharing, you will reap some fantastic benefits and blessings. You develop self-control gradually the way fruit grows and ripens on a tree. I didn't just wake up one day after giving my life to Christ and immediately have the ability to control my temper and my thoughts and my desires. It took time and effort, and I'm still working on it. I spent years on my knees in prayer and fasting and studying His Word. God has been faithful to transform and empower me by His Spirit as I sought to live by His Biblical principles and truth.

More important than the gifts of the Spirit are the fruit of the Spirit. Although the fruit of discipline and self-control is one of the hardest to develop, it is one of the most beneficial and rewarding.

Too often we only want to deal with the symptom, but God wants to deal with the root cause. Suppose there's a spider's web in the corner of your ceiling, and you sweep it down. Why is it that the next day it's back again? Because you didn't deal with the real problem. The problem is not the spider's web; the problem is the spider. Get rid of the spider and the web won't come back.

What is needed more than *instant deliverance* or some easy technique or formula that only deals with the symptoms, is a consistent life of discipline and self-control. Never forget, the essence of true strength, is self-control — being under His control!

As a person who was totally out of control, I'm telling you that if God can change me and bring my life under control and give me the physical, mental, and spiritual discipline and victory that He has, He can do it for anybody.

Dare to Be Different

Age of Conformity

We are living in an age of compromise and conformity. Many Christians seem to be no different from the world in this respect. They too are conforming to current popular trends in behavior and philosophy for no other reason than everyone else is doing it or believing it.

We must learn not to do things merely for acceptance or popularity. When others want us to do something that would cause us to violate our convictions, or is contrary to God's Word or the leading of His Spirit, we must have the courage to resist compromising and conforming. We must dare to be different!

Jesus Went against Tradition

Jesus had the boldness to go against centuries of tradition so that the truth of God's Word might be seen and obeyed. He insisted on showing love to those who were normally despised. For example, in John 4, He spoke to a woman in public which was not acceptable in that society. To make matters worse, she was a despised Samaritan. In Roman society, unwanted children were commonly disposed. Even His disciples took it for granted that He would not want to be bothered with them, yet He invited children to come to Him.

Pharisees recoiled from prostitutes, yet Jesus ministered to them and forgave them. Pharisees threw stones at untouchable lepers to make them keep their distance, but Jesus actually touched and healed lepers. In these and other ways, Jesus refused to compromise and conform to mere human custom. Whenever tradition went contrary to God's Word, Jesus honored God's Word.

Focus on the Lord

God has taught me not to model myself or my ministry after others. Sure, I gain insight and inspiration from the example of others and also learn from their mistakes. Nevertheless, God is the One who has instilled within me through His Word and Spirit His specific goals and purpose for my life and ministry.

As a new Christian, I tried to be like those I greatly respected. I tried to talk and act like them. I soon realized that God wanted to develop my own unique style and ministry. I had become so busy reading their books and getting their ideas that I had no time for His Word or prayer. When I began to seek the Lord's will and read His Word and obey it through the power of His Spirit, He gave me so many illustrations from my walk and adventures with Him that I can't possibly share them all. He began to use my life and ministry in ways I never dreamed possible.

A few years after a popular evangelist had a part in leading me to Christ, he left his family and ran away with his secretary. He became an alcoholic and got into trouble financially. If I had built my Christian life on him instead of on the Solid Rock, Jesus Christ, then I, too, may have fallen away from the Lord. I learned as a young Christian to seek to pattern my life after the Lord, and to keep my focus on Him and not on people — no matter how popular they are.

It does not matter how noble and Christ-centered a believer may be. If we keep our eyes on that person, they will eventually fail us. That is one reason why Ephesians 5:1 tells us to be imitators of God and why Romans 8:29 indicates that we are to be conformed to the likeness of Jesus Christ. When we keep our eyes on the Lord, we won't give up just because another Christian we respect happens to fall.

Don't Be a Clone

It appears that most people start ministries in one of two ways. They look around and see what is proving successful for other ministries and then they try to copy it, or they get on their knees and use God's Word to earnestly seek the Lord's will for the specific ministry He has for them, to fill a special need in the body of Christ.

Christians who are clones of others never realize the unique purpose and potential God has for them. Ministries that merely imitate and duplicate other ministries are usually superficial and lack the conviction and intensity of those who have been genuinely called of God. While all ministries should be similar in the sense that they are Christ-exalting and proclaiming Biblical Christianity, God has a special and unique plan for each of us in the body of Christ, if we will only seek His will.

Because I sought the Lord and didn't let others determine what my ministry should be or do, while others came and went, our ministry continued. While others rode the wave to temporary fame and popularity, ours continued to steadily grow. We earnestly attempted to build our ministry from day one on His Word and the leading of His Spirit, and as a result, He has greatly blessed it.

Be Unique

Don't be jealous or envious of what God is doing through someone else or another church or ministry. If the Jesus of the Bible is being exalted and His Kingdom is being truly advanced, then rejoice!

God has made you unique in your physical appearance; no two people even have the same fingerprints. God has also given you special talents, gifts, and abilities. Instead of being jealous or comparing yourself to others, use what He has given you for His glory. Remember, when we seek to be conformed to the likeness of Christ and truly desire to walk in obedience to His will, we fulfill the unique calling and purpose He has for us!

Courage to Stand Alone

Daniel Taken into Captivity

Daniel was taken captive to Babylon as a youth. He was separated from his family and friends. In that difficult situation Daniel determined that he would honor the God of the Bible.

In Daniel 6, the Persians, having overthrown the Babylonians, were in control. Daniel was much older. King Darius appointed Daniel as one of three administrators over his kingdom with 120 governors under them. The other two administrators were jealous of Daniel, so they tricked King Darius into making a decree that anyone who prayed to any god or man other than the king during the next 30 days would be thrown into the lion's den. Daniel 6:10 says —

> Now when Daniel learned that the decree had been published, he went home to his upstairs room where the windows opened toward Jerusalem. Three times a day he got down on his knees and prayed, giving thanks to his God, just as he had done before.

Imagine being taken captive to a distant land

where everyone around you is involved in occult practices. You are told that if you read your Bible, pray in Jesus' name, or witness you will be cast into a cage of hungry, ferocious lions. Think about the fear and emotional duress you would experience and the courage it would require for you to violate that decree.

That's the situation Daniel faced. Those who tricked King Darius into making the decree spied on Daniel, knowing that he would continue to faithfully pray.

All Daniel had to do was postpone his prayers for 30 days or at least close his windows. He had too much integrity to close the windows, and continued his regular procedure of honoring his God by courageously praying and seeking the Lord's help.

My Crisis-Oriented Relationship

There was a time before committing myself to Christ when I only wanted God's involvement in my life when I was in trouble and needed His help. Then I would get very spiritual. As a teen I would get out a Bible and lay my hands on it, and I would say, "Oh God, if you get me out of this mess, I'll change." Once the crisis passed, so did my commitment to the God of the Bible. It was superficial. I only had a "crisis-oriented" relationship. When I was in a crisis, I wanted God's help. When everything was going well, I didn't want Him interfering with my life.

Daniel did not have a crisis-oriented relationship with God. He had already been praying three times a day. Therefore, when the decree went out, Daniel didn't panic; he didn't fall apart and lose his composure. If you want boldness, courage, strength, and power, then follow Daniel's example. Daniel consistently honored God throughout his life, and God honored and greatly blessed him. I Samuel 2:30 accurately says, "... Those who honor Me I will honor, but those who despise Me will be disdained."

Daniel 6:16-23 gives the following account —

So the king gave the order, and they brought Daniel and threw him into the lion's den. The king said to Daniel, "May your God, whom you serve continually, rescue you!"

A stone was brought and placed over the mouth of the den, and the king sealed it with his own signet ring and with the rings of his nobles, so that Daniel's situation might not be changed.

Then the king returned to his palace and spent the night without eating and without any entertainment being brought to him. And he could not sleep.

At the first light of dawn, the king got up and hurried to the lions' den. When he came near the den, he called to Daniel in an anguished voice, "Daniel, servant of the living God, has your God, whom you serve continually, been able to rescue you from the lions?"

Daniel answered, "O king, live forever! My God sent His angel, and He shut the mouths of the lions. They have not hurt me, because I was found innocent in His sight. Nor have I ever done any wrong before you, O king."

The king was overjoyed and gave orders to lift Daniel out of the den. And when Daniel was lifted from the den, no wound was found on him, because he had trusted in his God.

The men who had plotted against Daniel along with their families were thrown into the lions' den and killed (Daniel 6:24), while Daniel was protected and greatly prospered (Daniel 6:28).

Sometimes We Feel All Alone

Throughout Scripture, we discover that living for God requires believers to occasionally stand alone — as did all of the great Biblical heroes.

Joseph was thrown into a pit by his brothers. He

was all alone, rejected, and sold as a slave into Egypt. In Egypt, because he honored God and spurned the affection of Potiphar's wife, he was thrown into prison. Nevertheless, Joseph continued to honor the Lord and eventually God exalted him to the second highest position in Egypt, and used him to save his family from starvation.

Moses had a chance to enjoy all the riches of Egypt for a season. Instead, he chose to reject them. As a result, he wandered in the dry and barren Midian desert. Eventually he was greatly used by God to lead Israel out of Egyptian bondage. Hebrews 11:25,26 says of Moses —

> He chose to be mistreated along with the people of God rather than to enjoy the pleasures of sin for a short time. He regarded disgrace for the sake of Christ as of greater value than the treasures of Egypt, because he was looking ahead to his reward.

David went out alone to meet the giant Goliath. David's situation seemed hopeless, yet he won because the Lord was with him. David desired to honor the God of the Bible, and shut the mouth of Goliath who was mocking the Lord and intimidating the whole army of Israel. His attitude was one of confidence and faith in the Lord as seen in I Samuel 17:37 —

> The Lord who delivered me from the paw of the lion and the paw of the bear will deliver me from the hand of this Philistine ....

David was willing to put his life on the line. He had been prepared for this feat by taking on a lion and a bear. David had all the odds against him: his opponent was bigger and stronger, his oldest brother Eliab opposed him, and even King Saul told him he wouldn't be able to do it. His only weapon was a sling and five smooth stones, but David was courageous because he knew God was with him. As a result, he accomplished one of the most memorable feats in

Scripture, and he is remembered as one of the great heroes of the Bible.

Consider Elijah, a prophet of God, who had an encounter on Mt. Carmel against hundreds of prophets of Baal. Although he was a notable minority, God honored Elijah's stand and his courage by consuming the sacrifice with supernatural fire from heaven.

The Apostle Paul could have become discouraged and given up when everyone forsook him and he had to endure persecution alone. Nevertheless, bravely he stood for Christ, empowered by the Holy Spirit.

You read about all these great Bible heroes and desire to be like them. So do I. And God speaks to my heart, "Then you'll go through the same training program that I put them through, if you want what I did in their lives."

All the Bible heroes had to one day stand alone. God is calling you to develop your spiritual muscles, because one day you may have to stand alone for your testimony for Jesus Christ and the Word of God. Following the crowd is not always the best way to go. In Scripture the crowd is often wrong, and the one standing alone is often the one honoring the Lord.

You Won't Be Standing Alone

When I played football, or I should say, tried to play football, there was a sign in the locker room which read:

> Courage is not lack of fear, but standing your ground in spite of it.

When I used to read about Bible heroes and their feats, like David against Goliath, I didn't imagine their hearts beating faster or their breathing rate increasing the way ours do when we get into confrontations. I mistakenly thought they had no fear when they had to stand alone for the God of the Bible.

God showed me through His Word, however, that

they had the same emotional responses we have. Their faith in God overcame their fear, and each one stood in spite of having a rapid heartbeat, accelerated breathing, and wanting to escape. They went out in faith and confidence and God empowered them.

Courage is not lack of fear. Courage is standing your ground for the Lord in spite of your fear.

I know it's convenient to compromise and conform in order to be popular and have everyone like you. But if you want God to use you in a great and special way, then you need to allow the God of the Bible to give you supernatural courage.

Sometimes you might have to resist conforming and compromising, and you might have to stand alone. Scripture promises that you really won't be standing alone, "Never will I leave you; never will I forsake you" (Hebrews 13:5). Besides, "If God is for us, who can be against us?" (Romans 8:31).

90-Foot-High Golden Image

In Daniel chapter 3, we read about King Nebuchadnezzar, who had just erected a 90-foot-high golden image and decreed that at the sound of the musical instruments everyone was to bow down and worship it. Then he had all the leaders gather in Babylon. They were all prepared to do what King Nebuchadnezzar had commanded; otherwise, they would forfeit their lives.

Shadrach, Meshach, and Abednego were the only ones who refused to bow down. Here is what they said to King Nebuchadnezzar when their lives were on the line —

> "O Nebuchadnezzar, we do not need to defend ourselves before you in this matter. If we are thrown into the blazing furnace, the God we serve is able to save us from it, and He will rescue us from your hand, O king. But even if He does not, we want you to know, O king, that we will not serve your gods or

worship the image of gold you have set up!" Then Nebuchadnezzar was furious with Shadrach, Meshach and Abednego, and his attitude toward them changed. He ordered the furnace heated seven times hotter than usual (Daniel 3:16-19).

It was so hot that the king's valiant warriors who were escorting the young Hebrew men to the fiery furnace were consumed by the heat. Scripture indicates that God protected Shadrach, Meshach, and Abednego because of their faith and courage. They could have compromised and conformed. They could have easily made excuses and justified bowing down, but they chose to remain standing while all the multitudes of people bowed their knees to worship. God delivered them from the fiery furnace and greatly honored them.

New Testament Examples of Courage

After Paul, accompanied by Barnabas, healed a crippled man in Lystra (Acts 14:8-10), the people wanted to offer sacrifices to them, thinking them to be gods. But Paul and Barnabas refused (Acts 14:11-18).

Yet, in spite of the intensity of the town's infatuation with Paul and Barnabas, their popularity was short-lived, and Paul was stoned in Lystra (Acts 14:19). Paul miraculously recovered and went immediately back into the city of Lystra. He stayed there until the next day (Acts 14:20). Time after time Paul returned to cities where people had previously tried to kill him.

Why did Paul keep returning to these cities when he knew to do so would be life threatening? He returned to strengthen and encourage the new disciples (Acts 14:21-23). What boldness and courage he exhibited in doing the Lord's work! That's the kind of courage I want.

Consider the courage of Stephen as he boldly spoke in the power of God's Spirit to the Jewish

Sanhedrin even though it cost him his life. Acts 7:51-60 states —

"You stiff-necked people, with uncircumcised hearts and ears! You are just like your fathers: You always resist the Holy Spirit! Was there ever a prophet your fathers did not persecute? They even killed those who predicted the coming of the Righteous One. And now you have betrayed and murdered Him — you who have received the law that was put into effect through angels but have not obeyed it."

When they heard this, they were furious and gnashed their teeth at him. But Stephen, full of the Holy Spirit, looked up to heaven and saw the glory of God, and Jesus standing at the right hand of God. "Look," he said, "I see heaven open and the Son of Man standing at the right hand of God." At this they covered their ears and, yelling at the top of their voices, they all rushed at him, dragged him out of the city and began to stone him.

Meanwhile, the witnesses laid their clothes at the feet of a young man named Saul. While they were stoning him, Stephen prayed, "Lord Jesus, receive my spirit." Then he fell on his knees and cried out, "Lord, do not hold this sin against them." When he had said this, he fell asleep.

Stephen's death no doubt impacted Paul's life later on. Acts 8:1 says —

And Saul was there, giving approval to his death. On that day a great persecution broke out against the church at Jerusalem, and all except the apostles were scattered throughout Judea and Samaria.

Bold in the Lord

When I was still relatively new in ministry, I went to hear a former motorcycle gang member and martial arts champion speak at a Christian businessmen's banquet. A teenage girl from a rough background came with one of my female staff to hear him speak. The teenager was telling my staff member how much she liked what he was saying, but the speaker thought she was acting smart and not listening. He pointed a finger at her accusingly and said, "I've had enough of you and your interruptions!" He publicly humiliated her. She got up and stormed out — totally turned off to him and Christianity.

Most of the Christians at the dinner were afraid to confront him, but afterwards my wife and I, along with the staff member, went back to talk to this huge guy. We met him outside as he was leaving. I told him, "I don't think you used wisdom in dealing with the teenage girl. You're trying to scare people into accepting Christ. You're using your size and your background to scare them so they won't talk back to you, but you don't need to use that kind of strategy. You need to deal with your pride, because you're coming across with a very egotistical attitude."

He became hostile and irate. His eyes blazed as he snarled, "Who are you to dare question me? You've never walked in my shoes. You haven't been through what God has taken me through. No one has ever said the things to me that you are saying." I answered, "I don't care what anyone else has said to you. I know what God's Spirit is showing me. You have a problem with pride and you are using your size and your background to intimidate people."

I stood my ground as he moved toward me. I knew he wanted to hit me. He towered above me like a big, mean grizzly. Karen and the other woman were there, and I was concerned for their safety. He aggressively closed in on me, to deliver an ultimatum. Instead of violence he suddenly softened and said, "Brother, don't you see, the very things you're saying are what God is dealing with me about. That's why I'm so angry."

After that breakthrough we had a chance to really talk and share. The next night he came back to speak at a nearby location and his attitude was completely different. He gave an altar call and many people went forward — the response was great.

I feel we had an impact on his life. If only some fearless Christian or Christian leader would have confronted him long before, it could have saved him a lot of grief.

While ministering in Haiti, I met a Haitian pastor whose church was in the midst of a voodoo village. I explained to him that his name "Bill" means "bold protector." I told him, "We are not to be cowardly nor bashful, but bold. We are not to be cocky or boastful, but confident and courageous in the Lord. We must fearlessly minister for the Lord and stand for the truth of His Word empowered by His Spirit!"

Love Not Your Life unto Death

All the New Testament writers, with the exception of the Apostle John, were martyred for their faith. According to early Church tradition, Peter was crucified upside down, Paul was beheaded, James was thrown off the pinnacle of the temple in Jerusalem and then beaten to death with clubs, and John was thrown into a boiling cauldron of oil and exiled to the Isle of Patmos.

During early church history many Christians were tortured, burned at the stake, thrown to wild animals, and beheaded. Some were made to serve as objects of amusement. Others were clad in the hides of beasts and torn to death by dogs. Some were crucified. Others were set on fire to illuminate the night. It is said that Emperor Nero had Christians set afire as human torches to light his gardens.

Hebrews 10:32-39 says —

> Remember ... when you stood your ground ... in the face of suffering. Sometimes you were publicly exposed to insult and persecution; at other times you stood side by side with those who were so

treated. You sympathized with those in prison and joyfully accepted the confiscation of your property, because you knew that you yourselves had better and lasting possessions.

So do not throw away your confidence; it will be richly rewarded. You need to persevere so that when you have done the will of God, you will receive what He has promised. For in just a very little while, "He who is coming will come and will not delay. But My righteous one will live by faith. And if he shrinks back, I will not be pleased with him." But we are not of those who shrink back and are destroyed, but of those who believe and are saved.

I may one day die for Christ, but the Lord has assured me that my life will not be taken until His purpose is fulfilled. My prayer is, "Lord, let me have the grace, the power, the boldness, and the forgiveness of Stephen." (See Acts 6:8 - 7:60.)

I used to wonder why Peter, Paul, and other Bible heroes, as well as many believers throughout history, had to be martyred, and why I and others may one day have to give our lives for Christ. It seems like defeat. I thought a better testimony would be God supernaturally intervening and delivering His people, which He has sometimes done, but not always (Hebrews 11).

Later I came to understand that enduring suffering for Christ was a sign and a seal that indicated the authentic nature of their testimony. When the world observed their unwavering faith — even in the face of death — they were more prepared to believe the message of the witness because they had validated it with their lives.

In fact the Greek word for witness is *martus* or *martur* which means "one who bears witness by his death." This definition is evident in the lives of Peter, Paul, and others who lived and died what they believed.

God's Spirit transformed them. Peter, on the night of Jesus' arrest, cowered at the accusations of a slave girl, but after seeing the resurrected Christ he became the man who not only boldly witnessed for Christ in Jerusalem (the very city He was crucified in) but he also courageously gave his life for the Lord by being crucified upside down.

Leonard Ravenhill said, "He who fears God fears no man. He who kneels before God will stand in any situation."

Jesus said in Matthew 10:28 —

Do not be afraid of those who kill the body but cannot kill the soul. Rather, be afraid of the One who can destroy both soul and body in hell.

I would rather die living for the Lord, than live denying Him. It makes sense that if I have the courage to die for Christ, I must necessarily have the courage to totally live for Him as well!

God Transformed Me

God transformed me from a person who always conformed to peer pressure to one who refuses to compromise and conform. I have had to stand alone for the Lord frequently in spite of being mocked, ridiculed, threatened, and having my life in danger on numerous occasions. His Spirit has helped me stand strong under such great pressures and opposition.

God gradually changed my life. I didn't wake up the day after giving my life to Christ and suddenly have the courage and strength to stand alone. As I studied and obeyed His Word, His Spirit empowered me to live for Him — no matter what the cost.

Why does God allow all this peer pressure? God allows the peer pressure and obstacles we face to mold our lives, build our character, and make us strong and courageous for Him.

In my basement, I used to have a speed bag on the left, a 70-pound heavy bag on the right, and a double-ended striking bag in the center. I would work out on all three simultaneously using both hands and feet. I used to put myself through all kinds of rigorous training. Why? Because I wanted to rise above any situation in which I would find myself. So too, God allows us to face many obstacles and difficulties to help us grow strong and to keep us in shape spiritually. Then we can stand in any situation — no matter how great the pressure is being put on us.

Before I left the martial arts, one of the training exercises was to stand alone in a big circle of 15-20 people. The idea was that each student would have a number, but it would be staggered so the one standing in the middle wouldn't know from which direction an opponent would come. Then the instructor would call out a number. Whoever had their number called would attack the one in the middle with a strike or kick or a combination. When you were selected to be in the middle you had to block, then counterattack.

Opponents might come from any direction. You never knew where they were coming from — front, back, or side. This experience was to train us on how to deal with unexpected situations on the street. So it is in life. God is allowing the obstacles, opposition, and pressure to mold us, develop our spiritual muscles, and prepare us for what lies ahead.

Ultimate Peer Pressure

Revelation 13:8 gives the ultimate form of peer pressure and reveals where a spirit of compromise and conformity will eventually lead. It states, "All inhabitants of the earth will worship the beast [the Antichrist]." That's going to be the ultimate in peer pressure, conformity, and compromise. Deny or die! For all who refuse to worship the image of the

Antichrist will be killed (Revelation 13:15).

If you cannot resist the peer pressure now, then you'd better let God infuse you with His power, because there will come a day in the very near future when all of society will be in total rebellion against the Lord, and it will cost a high price to stand for Jesus Christ.

Revelation 21:8 says —

> But the cowardly, the unbelieving, the vile, the murderers, the sexually immoral, those who practice magic arts, the idolaters and all liars — their place will be in the fiery lake of burning sulfur. This is the second death.

"Why the cowardly?" Because out of fear for their life or loss of property the cowardly either refuse salvation though they are convinced of its truth, or they walk away from it in times of persecution. Those who conform and compromise, and don't depend on God to give them the courage and strength to stand up and make their life count, are, in His eyes, just as bad as the murderers and the sorcerers, also mentioned in this verse, who will have their place in the lake of fire.

God accepts no excuse for being cowardly and denying Him, like those who no doubt tried to justify why they compromised and bowed down to Nebuchadnezzar's golden image. Throughout the ages there has always been a remnant of God's people who have had the God-given courage and strength to remain standing, like Shadrach, Meshach, and Abednego. Remember, you can either stand alone *for* the Lord now, or one day stand alone *before* Him in judgment!

After graduating from Bible college, I took a position as a youth pastor in North Carolina. To supplement my income, I was employed by a small convenience store from 11 p.m. to 7 a.m, the graveyard shift, where I was working alone. To show how potentially dangerous this was, a man in a similar store just down the road a few miles had recently been robbed and shot to death. It was in this setting that a gang would come into my store from a neighboring city, spread out through the store, and shoplift. Some young men who often came into the store said, "Bill, when that gang comes in again, we are going to stand with you, and we'll get the stuff back." I said, "Okay guys, great. Let's do it."

Sure enough, the gang came when my buddies happened to be there. Like before, the gang went through the store and began to steal things. They paid for a few items and then walked outside with all the stuff they had stolen and got into their car. I said, "Okay guys, you told me if they stole again you'd stand with me. Let's go out there and get the stuff back."

One guy said, "Man, there are six of them and four of us!" He went back in the cooler to hide. The other guy went in the rest room and locked the door. The third guy sat there saying, "No way! There are too many of them, Bill." I replied, "Thanks guys!" and walked outside by myself. I knocked on their car door window and they rolled it down. "Guys," I said, "you stole some stuff, and I want it back." All four doors opened and the six of them got out and encircled me. There was no way in that close proximity that I could do anything to effectively defend myself. I was totally vulnerable.

I said again, "Guys, you stole some stuff and I want it back!" They looked at me, then at each other. They didn't know whether to attack me or what to do. Then all of a sudden they reached into their pockets, and began to pull out some of the merchandise. They threw it at me, got in their car, and drove off.

Don't be foolish or crazy, for that's tempting the Lord. But there comes a point in our lives when we can no longer compromise and conform, but we must stand for what is right and true.

The World Doesn't Need More Conformers

I used to speak at school assemblies on self-control, peer pressure, and courage. I would incorporate such demonstrations as kicking cigarettes out of volunteers' mouths, and other feats which illustrated my message. I often ended the assembly by having four volunteers come forward. One grabbed my right wrist, one grabbed my left wrist, one came from behind to grab me, and the other attacked from the front. Each one pulled me the way he wanted me to go. They wanted me to compromise, they wanted me to conform. When it appeared I would be pulled apart I would say "No!" as I quickly kicked all four of them, one after the other, leaving them lying at my feet. I did this to demonstrate that we must refuse to be victimized by peer pressure.

The world does not need wasted persons, burnouts, conformers, compromisers, or those who give in to all the peer pressure. There are already enough weak-kneed, cowardly people in the world, as well as in the Church today. What we do need are those with God-given courage to stand up and make their lives count. Instead of being influenced by the world, let's influence our world for Jesus Christ!

God Wants Champions

I was in prayer near the end of a seven-day fast, at which time the Lord gave me the following:

> The world does not need another Savior or Messiah. He has already come and He will be returning again soon. What the world needs are champions to stand up and face the modern day Goliaths with God given courage, faith, strength, power, and victory, and proclaim the true resurrected Messiah!

I want to be one of the Lord's champions who will do exploits in the last days, as Daniel (11:32) indicates. I want to be one who is mightily used by the Lord now (as a foreshadow of how He will use the two prophets in Revelation chapter 11).

Will you also allow the Lord to make you into one of His champions by being totally committed to Him and by walking in obedience to His Word and His Spirit?

In the age we are living, we need true believers in Christ who will:

- have God-given courage and strength
- dare to be different and make their lives count
- not compromise and conform, even in the face of extreme pressure and persecution
- stand alone, if need be, and totally live for the Lord!

Determination to Never Give Up

Are You a Wimp, a Whiner, or a Winner?

I used to run an event called the Ultimate R.I.O.T. (Ridiculous, Interesting, Outstanding, and Terrific) which involved hundreds of young people. Many said it was the most exciting competition they had ever experienced. During the Ultimate R.I.O.T., they participated in an obstacle course, chariot race, refrigerator box relay, giant pushball, tug of war, indoor snowball fight using stacks of newspapers rolled up into paper snowballs, and many other challenging contests.

I coordinated this for several years for various groups throughout the country. After the event I would evaluate the participants collectively as to whether they were wimps, whiners, or winners. I would explain that a wimp is someone who gives up; a whiner is someone who complains, blames others, or has a bad attitude; and a winner is someone who doesn't give up and has a good attitude no matter what.

Usually all the young people competed like winners. So when I shared my testimony at the end and spoke on peer pressure, I also encouraged them to live for the Lord the same way they competed in the Ultimate R.I.O.T. — with all their heart, and like winners who have determined never to give up.

Determination

All through my life, people frequently told me: "You can't do it! You're too young ... too small ... too weak ... too poor. You'll never make it. You might as well give up!" I was frequently told that what I planned to do was impossible.

So, as one who never really had much potential and was often considered the least likely to succeed, who would have thought that one day I would be leading an international outreach ministry which is impacting tens of thousands of lives.

What has made the difference in my life? I had one God-given characteristic in my favor — determination.

During my junior year of high school I went out for football. Some of my friends said I would quit after a few weeks. Although I was a rookie and inexperienced, I was determined to stick it out. Unlike basketball in junior high where I was cut after the first practice, in football no one was cut, you just quit. But I was determined to hang in there.

My coach began to notice that I was strong for my size. I weighed only 160 pounds but was able to bench press 250 pounds, so the coach would say to his upperclassmen players, "Look at Rudge, he's benching more than you big linemen." That didn't make me real popular with them. A few times they formed a circle around me during practice so the coaches couldn't see, and proceeded to hit me with their forearms and helmets and kick me with their practice spikes. But I wouldn't quit.

Even though I sat on the bench most of the time,

I still wouldn't quit. I didn't play any varsity my junior year and only about five quarters my senior year. Part of it was my fault because when the coach would put me in during practice, I wouldn't know the plays or I was skipping practice altogether due to chasing girls. I sealed my fate when I skipped a game for a party, and then realizing I might be thrown off the team, I drove alone to a game over an hour away, but I arrived too late to suit up.

The few games I did get in, after the defensive play was called in the huddle, I would have to ask another player what I was supposed to do. It was midway through my senior season when I got motivated to play, but by then it was too late. The coaches had given me chances, but I wasted them.

My main reason for going out for football was the physical conditioning. I guess I wasn't motivated enough to really want to play. My goal was only to stick it out, and that's all I achieved. You'll never go higher than your goals.

Years later, I sponsored a multi-media assembly at an area high school entitled *Champions*. Its basic message was that no matter what your circumstances or obstacles, if you have determination, you can be a champion. A true champion never gives up, never quits. Some of the film footage showed a Vietnam Vet who had both legs blown off, yet he refused to give up and became a weightlifting champion. The school principal told me that after viewing the media presentation, one of the worst students said, "Maybe there is still hope for me."

After the assembly, a teacher who was now one of the football coaches started walking down the aisle to the front of the auditorium towards me. I recognized that he was one of the big upperclassmen who had beat on me during football practice throughout my rookie year. My mind flashed back and I thought he was going to hit me upside the head and say, "You were a rookie then, and as far as I'm concerned you are still a rookie." But he walked up to me and told me he thought our assembly was one of the best ever.

When I began to lift weights in 7th grade, I was often told to quit wasting my time because I was too skinny and weak. The motivation that kept me going was my desire to become muscular like one of my older brothers. I wanted to overcome my puny physique because I was tired of being pushed around. My goal was to be the strongest in my class by the time I graduated.

Sometimes I had weightlifting partners and sometimes I had to work out alone. After many years of relentless training my weak-guy image was changing. My skinny body was developing muscles. When I graduated, pound for pound I achieved my goal, because I weighed only 160 pounds and was benching almost 300 pounds. Eventually, at age 18 I reached my benching maximum of 335 pounds, which back in 1971 was fantastic, especially for my weight of only 165 pounds.

When I started taking karate at the age of 17, I was told, "You'll never be any good at karate, Rudge. You're too muscle-bound from lifting weights. You're too tight. You have no control." They were right. I purposely had no control when sparring. By the second year, however, they were calling me Godzilla, because of my sparring ability and because I was the strongest and craziest in the class.

I'm not conveying this to brag, but to illustrate that by sheer determination we can do things thought impossible. How much more could we accomplish for the Lord if we would only be this determined and sold out for Him?

I graduated at age 17, which means I was always one of the youngest among my peers at school. I had to learn to fight to survive, but this adversity eventually turned out to be an advantage because it made me strong and determined.

When I became a Christian, many of my friends rejected me. They thought it was just another fad and wouldn't last. That was in May, 1971, and I'm still walking with the Lord.

When Karen and I ran away and got married, I was 18 and she was 17. I was only making $10 a week cutting grass. Almost everyone told Karen to get away from me and said our marriage wouldn't last a year. That was in June, 1971.

My wife and I arrived at Bible college with little money and no jobs. Very few people thought we would survive. Most of the other students were raised in church and knew much more about the Bible than I did. I struggled with things like who Paul was and how to locate the book of John. Many of my college classmates thought I'd never finish Bible college because I had cheated my way through high school. Yet I finished all four years, even though I had to work 40-60 hours a week, as well as attend classes and do homework. I also taught self-defense and exercise at the college and YMCA, and served as youth leader for a youth group. Ironically, many of the students who thought I'd drop out were the ones who never made it into ministry or later quit altogether.

In my senior year at Bible college, I had to change from night school to day school in order to fulfill the requirements for my degree. I had to quit my job at the window factory and find new employment. I chose to work for a financial services company selling investments and insurance. During an extensive training program, all the other trainees bragged how great they would be and how much they would sell. I kept my mouth shut and quietly planned my strategy. At the end of the training program, a vote was taken on who would be the most likely to succeed and who would be the least likely to succeed. The guy with the biggest mouth, the one who bragged the most about how great he was going to be as a salesperson, was voted most likely to succeed. I was voted least likely to succeed.

Yet within three weeks at the state convention, in front of hundreds of people, I was the only one from our class to be promoted to area manager. I would receive commissions from many of those trainees who had voted me least likely to succeed. Less than a year later — by the time I graduated from college — I was the only one from that training program still working for the company.

In August of 1977, with literally no money, no staff, and no facilities — just a lot of God-given determination — Karen and I started this ministry in the upstairs apartment of my parents' home. I used the kitchen table as my desk and Karen kept the ministry records in a file cabinet in our bedroom. Very few people thought we would succeed. Many said, "Others have tried and failed, and so will you." But with God's help we persevered.

The ministry was less than a year old and just starting to really get going when I broke my ankle in a freak accident at one of our teen outreaches at a local roller rink. I was carrying a chair while wearing skates when I tripped. Not wanting to break the chair, I crossed my legs and sat down. I knew I was in trouble when I reached down and straightened up my foot and it fell limp to the side from the weight of the skates.

I was in the middle of the rink. Pain began to surge through my body, but I sat there long enough to introduce the guest speaker. The young people thought I was putting on an act to be funny, so they were all laughing and clapping. When I finished the introduction, some of them realized something was wrong by the painful expression on my face and came over to help carry me out. Karen and a staff member transported me to the hospital. I thought they would put a cast on me and send me home. I was shocked when the doctor said, "You're going to have to stay here."

I had to have extensive surgery and be hospitalized a week. It appeared the ministry would end abruptly because it would wipe us out financially, since I did not have hospitalization. Karen and I were paying many of the ministry bills from the secular job I was working on the side. Besides, much of our ministry at that time was based on my leading recreation, fitness classes, and doing self-defense clinics and demonstrations in schools and churches.

In the past I had fallen many times doing various physical feats but had never been injured. And then just carrying a chair while walking with skates on, I tripped, causing one of the worst breaks the doctor said he had ever seen — other than from severe car wrecks.

During the surgery the doctor had to put a seven-inch rod in one side of my ankle and into the bone marrow of my leg, and wire in the other side of my ankle. Twice my cast turned red and had to be changed because of the bleeding following the surgery.

The day I was released from the hospital I was scheduled to speak for the college from which I graduated. The doctor discouraged me from traveling so far, but did allow it. It was the first time the college had asked me to speak since my graduation. I accepted the engagement previous to my accident, and I don't like to cancel when I make a commitment. I had Karen drive me three hours to the college. I had to sit preaching with a pillow under my leg which was elevated on a chair. The pain was extreme, but I endured it. The response to my lecture by students and faculty was very good and made the trip worthwhile.

I was determined to strengthen my ankle and keep in shape. Even in the hospital bed I began to move my toes in the cast. I forced myself to stand on crutches and walk the halls even though the pain was excruciating. I did this years before it was recommended to be up and moving right after surgery. When I got home I would lay in bed or on the floor and use dumbbells, or go outside and hobble on my crutches to the swing set to do pull-ups and hop on one foot up the steps on the swing set to do dips. I also designed various exercises to strengthen my ankle and leg — long before physical therapy became popular.

After the cast was removed, the doctor said I wouldn't be able to walk without crutches for several weeks. I asked him, "Doc, will I be able to play football and do karate kicks again?" He looked at me and said, "I don't know, could you do it before?" I kept exercising and strengthening my leg. The doctor was surprised how fast I recovered and was able to walk into his office without crutches — only using a cane — in less than a week after having the cast removed.

Instead of destroying me as I initially thought, these circumstances became a great blessing and victory. The advantage of that near disaster was that it increased my determination — that no matter what happened — God would always make a way, and I was never to give up.

When we desperately needed larger facilities for our expanding ministry, it appeared there was no possible way that we could ever afford them. However, God moved in a very special way and the land was donated.

Almost everyone said there was no way we could build without a bank loan, but we knew that God is faithful to fulfill what He leads us to do. In obedience to His will, we stepped out on total faith as we began, continued, and finished our facilities without a cent of interest being paid. The dream and goal that God had given us became a reality. The Lord was greatly glorified because we dared to trust Him to overcome what plainly seemed to be insurmountable obstacles.

The new president of the college from which I had graduated called to book me to speak there. During our phone conversation, he told me that back in 1975 (when I was fresh out of Bible college), the pastor of the church in North Carolina where I was youth pastor said to him, "Bill just doesn't have ministry in him, and I advised him to give it up." Now years later, the president of my alma mater was asking me to address the student body on *The Impossible* and how we had developed such a successful ministry. Isn't it amazing how things change?

There are many other illustrations I could share of how God has enabled us to accomplish that which others thought was impossible. In reality, however, people were right thinking that I didn't have much potential. But I have built my life and ministry on Philippians 4:13, "I can do all things through Him who strengthens me" (NAS). Has it proven true? God took a young kid from the West Hill of Sharon, Pennsylvania, who had no hope or potential, and He has done *the impossible* through my life and ministry.

One of the reasons why we have such faithful volunteers and supporters for our ministry is they know I'm going to do what I say I'm going to do. If I believe God has led me to do something, nothing and no one will stop me. I will continue and I will endure until it is done. My procedure is to seek God's will for my life and ministry, then to have the determination to never give up until the Lord either fulfills what He led me to do or gives definite, new direction.

Most everything I have learned and done has not come easily. I guess my best degree is from the "school of hard knocks." That is how God has built my determination. Sure, I have been knocked down many times, but God has always given me the strength and determination to get back up again. I have realized that real failure is not when you fall, it is when you lie there and give up.

I have always enjoyed a challenge. It seems the more obstacles I face and the more opposition I receive, the more determined I become. Countless times throughout my life and ministry, I have had to face the cold reality that circumstances said, "You can't do it," and people kept reminding me, "You'll never do it," but God's Word said, "I can do all things through Christ who strengthens me." The Lord has instilled within me the mentality of never giving up — it's death or victory. No surrender and no retreat!

To have the determination to never give up, you must have goals, dreams, and vision based on Scripture. Believe that through Christ you can do it. Be willing to pay the price at all cost, and be motivated and empowered by His Spirit to persevere.

What is Your Dream?

What goals and vision has the Lord given you through study of His Word and prayer? If you don't have any, then spend time in Scripture, prayer, and fasting, and God will put His goals, His dreams, His vision, and His desires in your heart. One of the reasons I'm still in the ministry and still excited is due to my goals and vision for the future. As soon as I achieve one goal, God gives me two or three more. That keeps me motivated.

I often pray to the Lord: "Put Your thoughts and attitudes in my mind, and Your emotions, desires, goals, dreams, and vision in my heart. Give me unwavering faith to believe You and the motivation and determination to persevere."

Motivation

You can accomplish almost anything if you are motivated.

When my daughter was a one-and-a-half-year-old toddler, I was in my senior year at Bible college. It was close to graduation, so we sold our mobile home and were living in a former teacher's house on campus. Someone was supposed to be watching our daughter Tabitha. Suddenly I felt compelled to look out the second-floor window, and saw that she was playing in the middle of the road in rainwater and mud. The road had a sharp curve which would obstruct a driver from seeing that anyone was in the road — especially a little one-and-a-half-year-old who was sitting down. If a car had come it would have smashed her little body. I had already lost a seven-year-old brother who had been hit by a car, so I was motivated to respond quickly.

I jumped down one flight of steps, turned 180° and then jumped down another flight. In my haste I forgot about the low ceiling at the bottom of the steps. My forehead hit the ceiling and split open. The impact was so hard it bent the metal covering and threw me back so that my lower back hit the front edge of the steps. But I was motivated and nothing was going to stop me from getting to her — not even the dazed and disoriented state I was in, nor the blood which was now oozing over my head and face. I got up and ran directly to Tabitha, scooped her out of the road and brought her back inside. It was only then that I discovered how much my head and back hurt.

The point is this: I had one goal in mind — get Tabitha out of that life-threatening situation and back to safety — and I had one motivation — my overwhelming love for my daughter. We must have not only a vision but also the motivation which stirs us to action.

Develop a Persevering Attitude

My mentality is such that I am not going to give up until I accomplish the goal. For example, almost every summer I would cut down weeds and get poison ivy. Normally I would go to the doctor for medication. If it was serious enough, he would give me a shot.

During the summer of 1982, my oldest brother and I were cleaning out brush on the ministry property. It included a lot of poison ivy. We were wearing gloves as we were cutting it down to protect us. Then we burned it, not realizing that smoke from burning poison ivy can cause you to break out with a rash also. The rash began to spread all over my body.

Tired of getting poison ivy, I was motivated to endure it and build up my body's resistance against it. I didn't know how accurate this was medically, but it made sense to me at the time. All I did was take extra immune building vitamins and put on calamine lotion. I went to a local fitness center to take a steam bath, but it was not working that day. Thank the Lord it wasn't, for later I learned that it would have spread even more.

As any loving husband would do, I gave it to my wife. So we both were super itchy, but determined to beat it. It took two weeks, but it finally went away and I haven't had problems with it since. I think my body is afraid to get it again, because it knows what I may make it go through.

The above illustration might be a little unusual or whimsical, but the point is that we need to develop an attitude that we're never going to give up. God wants us to have a persevering spirit. To be motivated enough to endure until we accomplish His purpose and achieve victory.

Even before I gave my life to Christ, I had determination. When I wanted to achieve something, I would not quit until I dropped. When I wasn't motivated, I would get bored quickly and give up. That's why I quit job after job and relationship after relationship. As a teen I wasn't motivated to do very much except lift weights, practice karate, and have a good time.

After hitchhiking across the country at the age of 18, searching for answers to life, I had an encounter with the resurrected Christ. I found the answers in Jesus Christ. He gave my life purpose and meaning. He was someone to whom I could totally and completely dedicate my life. He has increased and redirected my determination and kept me motivated all these years. That is why He has accomplished through me what others thought was impossible.

Instilling Determination in My Children

I have sought to instill this same kind of Biblical determination in my children. My son, B.J., started playing soccer at age 6. He didn't like to practice nor did he see the importance of it. All he wanted was the excitement and challenge of the game and scoring goals. I knew if he was going to be good and achieve his potential he had to train.

I made him practice every type of kick imaginable using both feet. I made him run laps and do various drills I would invent. I made him practice soccer in the rain, mud, and snow. Above all I sought to teach him the importance of honoring the Lord and having a good attitude. B.J. became so motivated and dedicated that he would train two to three hours on his own almost every day.

The fruit of his labor paid off. By age 14, he had excelled in ability and was going to Europe with Team USA. Five days before he was to leave for Europe, he broke his ankle trying out for the Keystone State Games — which he made. After his recovery from ankle surgery, he paid the price by training harder than ever, and as a result went to Europe in 1992 with the East–West Soccer Ambassadors. He was made team captain and scored the most goals for the U.S. team.

He tore the anterior cruciate ligament (ACL) and did other damage to his right knee during the summer before his senior year of high school. After extensive rehabilitation, he came back to play for his team. After reinjuring his knee in another game, he had to have reconstructive surgery and was out for the season. In spite of physical setbacks, he came back to qualify for a scholarship at Geneva College. They won the national championship his freshman year. A week before the championship game, he completely tore the ACL in his other knee. After another surgery he did extensive rehabilitation and again came back. At the age of 18, he became a high school assistant soccer coach, and at age 19, he became one of the youngest head soccer coaches in the country.

A soccer coach from a rival team wrote in our local paper concerning him: "B.J. Rudge has the magic touch with a soccer ball that I have never seen before around Mercer County."

Sure it was hard, but he'll tell you it was well worth it. Even though over the years he faced many obstacles and injuries, he always persevered, and as a result won many honors and awards from his soccer skills — and also trained and impacted many others as well.

During track season, my daughter Tabitha was team captain in her senior year of high school, and improved each week. By the end of the season she was running times that seemed impossible for her just weeks before. Her determination and intensive training was motivated by three goals she developed for districts: break the school record in the open 800 meter, qualify for state, and at least place 3rd to receive a plaque.

All season long I had been encouraging her before the race with Isaiah 40:31 —

> But they that wait upon the Lord shall renew their strength; they shall mount up with wings as eagles; they shall run, and not be weary; and they shall walk, and not faint (KJV).

She was fantastic in the 800 meter relay at districts, and we were confident she would do well in the open 800. But it was not to be. She ran the 800, just missing the school record by a fraction of a second. She missed qualifying for state competition by two seconds, and she took fourth place, so she did not receive a plaque.

Tabitha was crushed. To make matters worse, the following day there was a big picture in the local paper's sports section of the 800-finish line. All season when Tabitha was winning, or at least placing, the pictures were of other track events, but this first picture of the 800 meter had a great close-up of the finish line, and showed only the first three place winners.

Tabitha had honored the Lord all season, and we just couldn't understand why the Lord brought her so far and then let her fall short of her goal. I said to Tabitha, "First, we have to get a proper perspective on this. Don't focus on missing the state meet, but focus on the fact that you are number four in the district which is quite an accomplishment." Then I told her, "Honor the Lord in this valley, and there will be a mountaintop coming up soon."

The next night Tabitha sang with the community choir at a large church in the area. I was way in the back and Tabitha was up front on the platform singing, but we simultaneously looked at each other as they sang one of their new songs, *They That Wait Upon the Lord.*

The founder of this interracial and highly

successful choir selected Tabitha and another young man to help him take the offering. But before he did and unknown to Tabitha, he spent several minutes sharing how Tabitha was instrumental in getting this tremendous choir started and how she has really lived the life and influenced many to come to Christ. It wasn't the way we expected, but God had honored her for honoring Him. While track is very important to Tabitha, her walk with the Lord is even more important.

Paul says in I Corinthians 9:24,25 —

> Do you not know that in a race all the runners run, but only one gets the prize? Run in such a way as to get the prize. Everyone who competes in the games goes into strict training. They do it to get a crown that will not last; but we do it to get a crown that will last forever.

At Geneva College, Tabitha faced additional obstacles, injuries, and sickness, but she persevered. She set two indoor track records — one her freshman year and one her senior year. She also placed 33rd at nationals (NCCAA) in cross country her senior year at Geneva (although she had never ran cross country before) and helped her team place fourth at nationals.

In her senior year, she placed 4th in the open 400 at NCCAA. Her 1600 meter relay team, which was undefeated in district, placed 2nd at nationals. And her Geneva College women's team took second at nationals. The Lord has also honored and blessed her in many other ways for her faithfulness to Him.

Pay the Price

In 1986, I started coaching my son's YMCA soccer team, the Strikers. We lost the first game to the Flash, an excellent team. So I gave the Strikers a choice. "Give up, or if you are willing to pay the price, I'll train you hard, and we'll go for it." They agreed to go for it, so I trained them hard. We developed an extensive training program and obstacle course at the ministry center, scrimmaging older and better teams, showing special training and motivational videos, and so on. We used Philippians 4:13, "I can do all things through Him who strengthens me" as our theme.

We won the rest of our games that year and also won the championship game. During the four years I coached we never lost another game, and our teams won both the league and playoff championships. Pay the price and the results will follow.

The last year I coached youth soccer, I designed a 15-station obstacle course. They had to dribble around cones, then pass under a net, head the ball over or under a volleyball net, shoot on goal, chip over a picnic table, pass through two wooden horses, take five speed shots against the back of our building, dribble around more cones, run tires, cross monkey bars, chip over a picnic table, shoot on another goal, chip through a suspended inner tube, jump over a heavy bag, and do ten rebound kicks against an inverted trampoline. Not only did it develop determination and endurance, but greatly helped them develop key soccer skills.

You Can Do It

At the end of regulation play of our championship game during my fourth year of coaching, we were tied 1-1. I wanted to play it out so we could win or lose as a team, but the other team's coach said, "No, we can beat you in a shoot-out." So I said, "Let's go for it."

I got my team together and said we need to pray for wisdom. I prayed and then I picked five shooters and the other team picked five shooters. We ended up with a tie again. I said to the other coach, "Let's play it out," but he said, "No, we can beat you in a shoot-out," so I said, "Let's go for it again."

I got the team together again and said, "We need

to pray again for wisdom. I chose five more players. The Lord impressed on my heart to choose one of my worst players. I only played him a few minutes during the whole championship game. My assistant coaches and the players looked at me as if to say, "You're crazy, coach!"

When the other team saw who I chose and was up to shoot, they started laughing and saying, "He's nothing, he can't do it!" Right before he shot, I went up and hit him on the shoulder and said, "You can do it!" He blasted that ball as hard as he could and it went right over the goalie and into the net, scoring the winning goal. We won the championship.

Don't ever tell me you can't do it. I'm the wrong person to say that to. If I could achieve all I have with no real potential, how much more for those of you who have been blessed with talents and abilities?

Not by Might

Zechariah 4:6 says, "... 'Not by might nor by power, but by My Spirit,' says the Lord Almighty." God has taken the bit of determination I had in my past and has redirected and increased it, and enabled me by His power to do what many people thought was impossible. In my records on *The Impossible* and *Adventures in Missions,* I document some of the many impossible situations the Lord has enabled us to overcome through unwavering faith in Him, obedient determination, and persistent perseverance.

We Need Endurance and Perseverance

During my senior year at Bible college, I worked as an area manager for an insurance and financial investment company. I was out on an appointment with Oscar, a new man I was training. It was his first opportunity to give the total sales presentation himself and he was bound and determined to make the sale. Somewhat nervously, and in a monotone voice, he shared his presentation for about five minutes when the client's small dog ran over and started biting his hand and pulling on his shirt sleeve. Oscar didn't want to lose his train of thought and momentum, so he kept right on talking, ignoring what was happening. A few minutes later the dog circled the room and came back and started to bite and pull at his pant leg, but once again Oscar ignored it and kept right on talking. The dog's owner, probably hoping we would hurry and finish, did nothing. Then the dog circled the room again and jumped on Oscar's leg.

Oscar, being so determined to make the sale, did not chase it away. After we were done and outside the house, Oscar hurriedly took off his boot, turned it over, and dumped out yellow liquid. The dog, when it was on his leg, had actually wet in his boot, but Oscar kept quiet in hopes of making the sale. If Oscar had this much determination just to make a sale (that we didn't even make), how much more should we as believers in Christ be determined in our commitment to serve our Lord?

My First and Last Race

Several years ago, Karen and I were with another couple at a recreation area. There was a night race and the three of them were running in it. The husband kept asking me to run too, but I had never run in a race. Finally I accepted his challenge, since I'm willing to try almost anything once. All the runners were dressed in shorts, tee shirts, and tennis shoes. I was getting interesting stares, since I was wearing street clothes. Jokingly I commented to the couple and Karen, loud enough so that the other runners could hear, that I was listed in *Runner's World* (a magazine name I thought I made up — but discovered it was actually the name of the premiere running magazine). I wondered why the other runners stared at me even more curiously.

I positioned myself near the front of the line thinking I needed all the advantage I could get — not realizing the best runners are supposed to take that spot.

It was a 5k (3.1 mile) race. We were to run halfway around the lake, and then return the same way. I was involved in various forms of exercise, but running was not my forte because of injuries, and because I thought it was too boring. I liked exciting adventures requiring short bursts of energy. I had never run more than a mile before, so this was going to be a great challenge.

Not to get trampled at the start of the race, my strategy was to get out fast with the pack. I stayed with them the first 50-100 yards and then quickly moved to the side of the road to continue at a much slower pace. During the race I wanted to stop many times, but I kept going — refusing to walk. I kept hoping to see the leading runners returning — at least knowing the halfway mark was not too far away.

It seemed like an eternity before the first runners began to pass me heading in the opposite direction. Finally I made it to the halfway mark and thought, "I've made it this far, I can make it the rest of the way." The friend we were with was still heading for the halfway mark when I passed her on the way back. She asked if I wanted to walk and I said, "No way!" My ankle and knees were now hurting, but I decided I was going to complete this race no matter what. As I ran I reviewed in my mind *10 Things the Lord Taught Me* from my *Fasting Prayer List*, which helped greatly.

Finally, I heard cheering and soon saw the lights by the finish area. The finish line wasn't far ahead. I completed the race and was told my time was very good for someone who had never run before.

Although half of the people beat me, I did manage to come in ahead of the other half — including Karen and our friend's wife. I paid the price for completing the race. The next three days my legs ached, but knowing that I would probably never run in a race again, and having gained a lot of respect for runners (especially my wife and daughter who ran in many more races, including a half-marathon — 13.1 miles), I was glad I had accomplished this goal.

The Apostle Paul likens our walk with the Lord as a race. In the same way an athlete must have determination to face and overcome obstacles and difficulties, so must we in living for the Lord. In Acts 20:24 Paul says —

> I consider my life worth nothing to me, if only I may finish the race and complete the task the Lord Jesus has given me — the task of testifying to the gospel of God's grace.

In Galatians 5:7, Paul asks —

> You were running a good race. Who cut in on you and kept you from obeying the truth?

In I Corinthians 9:24-27, Paul said —

> Do you not know that in a race all the runners run, but only one gets the prize? Run in such a way as to get the prize. Everyone who competes in the games goes into strict training. They do it to get a crown that will not last; but we do it to get a crown that will last forever. Therefore I do not run like a man running aimlessly; I do not fight like a man beating the air. No, I beat my body and make it my slave so that after I have preached to others, I myself will not be disqualified for the prize.

Paul says in Philippians 3:12-14 —

> Not that I have already obtained all this, or have already been made perfect, but I press on to take hold of that for which Christ Jesus took hold of me. Brothers, I do not consider myself yet to have taken hold of it. But one thing I do: Forgetting

what is behind and straining toward what is ahead, I press on toward the goal to win the prize for which God has called me heavenward in Christ Jesus.

Hebrews 12:1-3 admonishes —

Therefore, since we are surrounded by such a great cloud of witnesses, let us throw off everything that hinders and the sin that so easily entangles, and let us run with perseverance the race marked out for us. Let us fix our eyes on Jesus, the author and perfecter of our faith, who for the joy set before him endured the cross, scorning its shame, and sat down at the right hand of the throne of God. Consider Him who endured such opposition from sinful men, so that you will not grow weary and lose heart.

Never Give Up

Bigger guys used to always want to fight me. So I would say to them: "You want to fight me, that's fine. You knock me down, I'll get back up. You knock me out, when I come to I'm coming after you. You break my arm, I'll use the other arm. You break my leg, I'll crawl after you. I will not give up, I'll keep coming after you!" Most of them didn't want to fight after that. We must have this same determination in our commitment to Christ.

One of the most important admonitions — repeated over and over in Revelation and in many other Scriptures — concerns the Lord's imminent return and is an exhortation to endure, be faithful, hold on, overcome, persevere, and stand firm to the end. (See Revelation 2:10, 25, 26; 13:10; 14:12; 21:7; Matthew 10:22; 24:13; Luke 21:16-19; James 5:8.)

My desire is to turn the hearts of the people back to the Lord and motivate them to walk in endurance and faithfulness to Him until He returns. As believers in Christ we must have the attitude that no obstacle or opposition will cause us to give up in defeat. Instead, we must endure to the end in our commitment to Him. We must persevere, remain faithful, and never give up until the Lord fulfills what He leads us to do or He gives us definite new direction.

The Apostle Paul was in prison at Rome, knowing that his time on earth was about to come to an end. Yet with faith and determination he wrote these powerful words in II Timothy 4:6-8 —

> For I am already being poured out like a drink offering [he was about to be martyred], and the time has come for my departure. I have fought the good fight, I have finished the race, I have kept the faith. Now there is in store for me the crown of righteousness, which the Lord, the righteous Judge, will award to me on that day — and not only to me, but also to all who have longed for His appearing.

The Apostle Paul's commitment to Christ resulted in unwavering faith and determination — even to death. Ask God to instill in you the same kind of determination to never give up!

Root Out Hidden Sins

Many Christians are involved in what I call hidden sins — practices which are totally unacceptable to God. For many years I allowed subtle sins in my life that I thought were innocent and acceptable to God, so I justified and condoned them. But God desires that we clean up our lifestyles and our thought lives, and let Him root out our hidden sins.

Many Christians have attitudes and involvements that are contrary to God's Word, but they have done them for so long that the initial grieving of God's Spirit has worn off. They have become desensitized and are no longer convicted. They have become tolerant and no longer feel any remorse or guilt. They have somehow justified these actions since everybody else is doing it. As a result, they do not allow God's Word and Spirit to deal with them to free them from enslavement.

If you turn your shower water to freezing cold, it will be a tremendous shock to your system. But if you gradually turn the water cooler and cooler, your body conveniently adapts and you hardly notice the transition. So too, most people fall away gradually, becoming lukewarm and then cold toward the Lord without noticing it. Eventually they leave their first love.

If you are to live a disciplined and holy life by His power and in His presence, then you can no longer tolerate the sin in your life that He exposes by His Word and Spirit. Hebrews 12:1 encourages believers to "throw off everything that hinders and the sin that so easily entangles ...."

Hiding His Face because of Hidden Sin

If you persist in allowing hidden sins in your life, then the Lord is going to hide His face from you. Isaiah 59:1,2 says —

> Surely the arm of the Lord is not too short to save, nor His ear too dull to hear. But your iniquities have separated you from your God; your sins have hidden His face from you, so that He will not hear.

Ezekiel 39:23,24 says —

> And the nations will know that the people of Israel went into exile for their sin, because they were unfaithful to Me. So I hid My face from them and handed them over to their enemies, and they all fell by the sword. I dealt with them according to their uncleanness and their offenses, and I hid My face from them.

Let God Root Them Out

"The fear of the Lord is the beginning of knowledge" (Proverbs 1:7). "To fear the Lord is to hate evil" (Proverbs 8:13). We must let God expose and eradicate hidden sins. As David said in Psalms 32:1-5 —

> How blessed is he whose transgression is forgiven, whose sin is covered! How blessed is the man to whom the Lord does not impute iniquity,

and in whose spirit there is no deceit! When I kept silent about my sin, my body wasted away through my groaning all day long. For day and night Thy hand was heavy upon me; my vitality was drained away as with the fever heat of summer. I acknowledged my sin to Thee, and my iniquity I did not hide; I said, "I will confess my transgressions to the Lord"; and Thou didst forgive the guilt of my sin (NAS).

In Psalms 51:10-12 David cried out —

Create in me a clean heart, O God, and renew a steadfast spirit within me. Do not cast me away from Thy presence, and do not take Thy Holy Spirit from me. Restore to me the joy of Thy salvation, and sustain me with a willing spirit (NAS).

Five P's

During a time of fasting I recorded *Five P's* of why many — even ministers — compromise and sell out their relationship with Christ:

1) Pleasure (many opt for the *easy life* or get compromised in sexual immorality)

2) Popularity (they become people pleasers more than God fearers)

3) Power (wanting to control and impress people)

4) Pride (striving for positions of high standing and prestige)

5) Prosperity (desiring material wealth more than God's favor)

The Lord had previously given me another set of *Five P's*. He taught me that when we become rebellious, or allow willful, hidden sin in our lives, we lose the following *Five P's*:

1) We lose His protection. There is a wall of protection around believers that comes down when we involve ourselves in willful

sin and rebellion.

2) We lose His provision. His hand of blessing is removed.

3) We lose His peace. When we're not in right relationship with the Lord, we don't rest in the Lord and walk in His peace.

4) We lose the sense of His presence. There is nothing worse than losing His presence.

5) We lose His power. We wonder why our prayers aren't answered, why we don't have discernment, why we are powerless and ineffective, and why the end result is not victory.

God wants all five of these "P's" in our lives, but to have them we must repent of our hidden sins and make Him Lord over every area of our lives. We must not tolerate and justify hidden sins, saying, "Well, you know, I can't be perfect. Everyone has problems. So, I'm going to hold on to my jealousy, my gossiping, my gluttony, my lust, my .... I'm still going to keep watching my movies. I'm going to keep doing this or that, but I still love You Lord, and I still want to serve You."

God is saying, "I want to clean up your life. I want these *Five P's* restored."

When you allow God to root out the hidden sins:

1) He restores His protection. As God has protected my life on numerous occasions, I have assurance He will continue to do so, until His purpose is fulfilled. Therefore, I can stand up with the courage of Elijah and take on the prophets of Baal and not be afraid, because God will protect me. Even if I lose my life, I am eternally sheltered from the second death and ushered into His presence.

2) He restores His provision. He won't give you everything you want, but He will give you everything you need. As your selfish desires are replaced by delighting yourself in Him, He will give you the desires of your heart.

3) He restores His peace. This does not mean you won't have problems. I'm talking about living a lifestyle that regardless of what you face, God gives you an inner peace. Even though everything is chaotic around you, you can cope and deal with it because you know you are in right relationship with the Lord. He has everything under control and is working it all together for good.

4) He restores His presence. While the worst feeling you can have is losing the sense of His presence, the best feeling is walking in His presence.

5) He wants to manifest His power in our lives. I want to have God's genuine power in this age of counterfeits and compromise — power to resist temptation, power to love my enemies, and power to pray for those who persecute me. I want to see the hearts of the people turned back to the Lord as His Spirit brings deep conviction on them. I also want to see God do mighty works and miracles through my life, as I boldly proclaim His Word. I want to see His power manifest as He stretches forth His hand to heal, and perform miraculous signs and wonders (Acts 4:30).

Desire the Lord

Three Levels of Christian Life

There are three levels of commitment that most Christians go through. First is the *feelings level*, as I shared before. We have to grow beyond living by mere feelings and experiences. It's fine to see a little baby running around in diapers, but for a teen or adult who does not have a medical problem, to be wearing diapers would be totally ridiculous. So too, it's okay if you're a new Christian, but if you've been walking with the Lord for several years, it is unnatural and unhealthy to run around in the spiritual diapers of feelings and experiences. It's time to grow up.

Second is the *commitment level*. This is where we live by obedience and commitment, regardless of how we feel. It is where we do what God's Word says, what His Spirit directs — whether we want to or not.

Thinking commitment was the ultimate level, I lived that way for many years. But the Lord showed me there is more that He has for us — what I call the *desire level*.

While in Phoenix in the summer of 1988, I was reflecting on my relationship with the Lord and everything that had been happening: the Middle East where my family and I were caught in a potential hostage situation and all the trauma that was involved; the Oregon wreck in which the car my family and I were traveling in was totaled in a four-vehicle collision; the tire blowout and near-accident with the next rental car I was driving in Arizona. I was reflecting on these and other related incidences and asking the Lord why they were happening. He impressed on my heart these three levels of commitment, especially the third and *ultimate* dimension of our Christian life — the *desire level.*

The Desire Level

The desire level is where we have a passion, hunger, and thirst for the Lord more than anything else on earth. My relationship with Jesus Christ is more important to me and fulfills and satisfies me more than anyone or anything else — more than sex, power, wealth, or any other temporary pleasure this world has to offer. All else is inferior to knowing Him. I never want to lose His presence. I understand what the psalmist meant when he said, "Besides Thee, I desire nothing on earth" (Psalm 73:25 - NAS) and "As the deer pants for streams of water, so my soul pants for You, O God" (Psalm 42:1).

The Lord is saying to you, "I have a deeper dimension for you. I have something that will fulfill you more than anything you are seeking through all the hidden sins in your life."

Think about this. The greatest feeling in the world does not come from drugs or alcohol, from sex or pornography, from self-gratification and indulgences, or from anything else the world is offering. I've tried just about everything imaginable and I can assure you, the greatest feeling in the world comes from knowing everything is right between you and the Lord and desiring Him more than anything or anyone else. He will be your ultimate fulfillment! This is the *desire level* God wants to bring you to.

When you "love the Lord your God with all your heart and with all your soul and with all your mind and with all your strength" (Mark 12:30), you remove anything that takes you away from Him. Instead of pursuing a meaningless existence in a world that entices you, you desire to seek Him through prayer, fasting, and study of Scripture. As you do, the temporary pleasures of this world will dim in comparison to knowing Christ. You will desire His will for your life while longing for His Second Coming when He will rule and reign in righteousness and peace for all eternity!

Take the Challenge!

By His Word and Spirit, God has shown me that only those totally committed to Him will be able to endure what's coming on the world scene in these last days.

It is so crucial that if you want to not only stand, but also have greater power and victory than ever before, then you must be totally committed to Christ as Lord. Walk in obedience to His will. Be available, yielded, submissive, surrendered, and sensitive to His Spirit and Word. Walk in humility, meekness, and integrity before Him. Develop a balanced life — physically, mentally, and spiritually. Exercise discipline and self control. Dare to be different and have courage to stand alone for Him. Never give up! Clean out the hidden sins in your life and desire Him more than anything else.

These are some of the Biblical principles which have greatly molded my life and ministry. I hope and pray you have been challenged and motivated by them too, as have thousands of others. Start today to apply each of these truths to your lives. Dare to achieve the full potential and purpose God has for you and allow

Him to do *the impossible* through your life.

I challenge you to *reach your maximum potential in Christ* by determining in your heart to desire and then strive to practice the following:

1) Lord, I have examined the evidence and counted the cost, and I want to live totally for You!

2) I will not settle for a superficial relationship with You. I want You to be Lord over every area of my life!

3) I want to walk in obedience to Your will!

4) I want to be available, yielded, sensitive, submissive, and surrendered to You and fulfill Your goals and purpose for my life!

5) I want to walk in humility and meekness before You!

6) I want to live a life of integrity before You and the world!

7) I want to glorify You with every aspect of my life — physically, mentally, and spiritually!

8) I want to live a life of discipline and self-control!

9) I don't want to compromise and conform to the world, but will dare to be different and boldly stand alone if need be!

10) I want to walk in faith, determination, perseverance, endurance, and faithfulness, and never give up until I go home to be with You, or until You return!

11) I want everything right between us. Help me not to tolerate hidden sin!

12) I want You to be the ultimate source of

my fulfillment, and help me to desire
You more than anything or anyone else
on earth!

Thousands of *ordinary* people have accepted this
challenge and dared to earnestly apply these Biblical
principles to their lives. They have shared some
amazing accounts of what God has done in and
through them. Their changed lives are living
testimonies to the power of God's Word and Spirit. I
look forward to one day hearing from you concerning
how God's Word and Spirit have transformed and
impacted your life and conformed you more into His
likeness (Romans 8:29).